Light and Dark: Muslims in Italy

Light and Dark: Muslims in Italy

The journey and the meeting of two worlds

by

Michele Groppi

Vij Books India Pvt Ltd

New Delhi (India)

Published by

Vij Books India Pvt Ltd
(Publishers, Distributors & Importers)
2/19, Ansari Road
Delhi – 110 002
Phones: 91-11-43596460, 91-11-47340674
Mobile: 98110 94883
e-mail: contact@vijpublishing.com
www.vijbooks.com

Copyright © 2020, *Author*

ISBN: 978-93-89620-22-1 (Paperback)
ISBN: 978-93-89620-23-8 (ebook)

All rights reserved.

No part of this book may be reproduced, stored in a retrieval system, transmitted or utilised in any form or by any means, electronic, mechanical, photocopying, recording or otherwise, without the prior permission of the copyright owner. Application for such permission should be addressed to the publisher.

To Marta, Linda, mom and dad

Contents

Foreword	ix
Introductory Note	xiii
Introduction	1
Racism Made in Italy?	6
A Matter of Integration	29
Focus on Women, Second Generations, and Converts	49
Radicalisation and Terrorism	78
The Journey and the Meeting of Two Worlds	107
Italian Muslims and Italian Non-Muslims	112
Are We the Next France?	117

Foreword

A verse from the Koran teaches Muslims that trust is clearly distinguished from error, while another describes the presence of God as light on light. Another verse illustrates how God guides creatures far from error towards the Light. To the majority of believers and sensitive and intelligent people, including Muslims in history and in the world and in Italy, the interpretation of the meaning of the narration of the sacred text is intuitive and deductive of good and evil; it guides towards the common and superior Good.

Unfortunately, since last century, a subversive propagandistic movement has exploited an apologetic interpretation of some verses of the Koran, making them slogans that would justify a political ideology that claims to legitimise violence, ignorance, injustice, arrogance, barbarism, chaos. This radical and fundamentalist propaganda, which claims to absolutize thoughts and homologate humanity by killing both Westerners and Orientals, civilians and believers, destroying institutional venues, public entertainment spaces, places of cult and burial places, has cast a shadow over public security, peace, and the identity of a traditional civilisation and of various peoples who have been genuinely referring to Abrahamic monotheism for generations: Jews, Christians and Muslims. Such power-fuelled blackmailing!

The abuse and manipulation of the doctrine of a religion is only a mask for a revolutionary guerrilla of independence from the world order. They disguise themselves as Gandhi without having his great soul. Instead, they end up emulating Mao, Stalin or Hitler, killing elders, women and children, monks and teachers, Buddhists, Christians and Jews, as well as many Muslims. And they dare to say that they do it in the name of God and Islam! Shameless.

The cultural and political damage is enormous. Ignorance and superficiality about religion in general increase. With them, the mistrust towards devotees, simple practitioners, precepts and religious rites increases. While we try cloning a moderate, secular, progressive, liberal, reformed Islam, religious freedom rights are denied and walls of prejudice are being built. From Europe to the United States, the tone rises against Jews and Muslims, foreigners and immigrants, reviving visions of protectionism and "Defence of the Race"! So much dark!

Attempting to shed light and give hope, we are witnessing an increasingly important and interdisciplinary collaboration between sensitive institutional representatives, religious referents open to dialogue and coherent with the context of contemporary Western society, and university researchers capable of producing analysis and articulating readings on updates of perceptions and situations.

This is what the work by Dr. Michele Groppi does, with whom COREIS, the Italian Islamic Religious Community, and other associations of Muslims in Italy, have collaborated to make an inquiry into the perception and the seams of seeming opposing worlds: Italians and foreign citizens, Muslim and Christian believers, democratic and revolutionary politicians, integrated and radical voters, pacifists and terrorists. The good and the bad is often transversal. Perception and reality almost never coincide and, therefore, the results of this study allow us to have an objective picture of the amount of rigorous work that cultural openness warrants. In addition to the method of scientific fidelity and the intellectual honesty that inspires Dr. Groppi, one must recognise his quality to defuse the debate, favouring comparative research at a European and international academic level.

Always committed to building cultural and institutional bridges, we wholeheartedly support this publication and its analysis, because the latter is complementary to the duty religious Muslims in Italy and the world have to interact with representatives of other religious confessions and collaborate with institutions and the academic environment to safeguard civil dialogue and intellectual progress amongst peoples.

We hope that all this will be able to promote the lights of knowledge, respect and dialogue and to build the added value of an Italian Islam within the spiritual heritage of our history and society.

Thanks to Michele Groppi for favouring this encounter!

Yahya Pallavicini Imam,
President of COREIS,
Italian Islamic Religious Community

Introductory Note

Michele Groppi overflows with enthusiasm: equally to when he was playing on the volleyball court, this book also shows his energetic and passionate ability to commit. Words, like volley balls, highlight the desire to get involved by exploring the "parquet" of knowledge, envisioning strategies to tackle his research on Muslims in Italy.

The subject demonstrates courage, because it combines anxiety over a particular emerging threat seen in recent years, that is, Islamist terrorism, with the tendency to simplistically stereotype the causes of this phenomenon, which facilitate the identification of the culprit "in the other", in this case observant Muslims.

The paper takes us on a two-year journey through fifteen Italian cities, where the story of the encounter with hundreds of Muslims is the story line that summarises and explains such convoluted scenarios. Prose is often a mixture of journalism and science, which facilitates the understanding of pivotal points and, above all, avoids increasingly popular narratives that are not supported by data.

If something is needed, in fact, it is a calm and an impartial analysis of the phenomenon of terrorism to understand it in all of its dimensions, aware that the latter will last for a long time, even if it may change actors and organizational forms, being itself integral part of the type of hybrid model of war that the world is facing. And let's not deceive ourselves: Italy is not immune to threats simply because, so far, it has not suffered attacks like other European countries.

Rightly, Groppi, in his final reflections, writes: "If not addressed, these potential challenges could promote a future of uncertainty. We could find ourselves with alienated generations of young Muslims residing in the new Italian banlieues, which, given our record of jihadism, could become venues of radicalisation and terrorism". In the book, in fact, a series of vulnerabilities are listed, which, when considered together, explain the basic discomfort that facilitates radicalisation and adherence to a false religion of death, as a response to everyday forms of alienation and deprivation: our task is to grasp these signs of vulnerability, which might be insignificant signs if taken in isolation, but could become dangerous if ignored. We are in a world that requires, for the latter to be governed, more and more knowledge; what a pity that, way too often, on the contrary, we abandon ourselves to the dramaturgical representation of such phenomena, shifting political actions by governments to shamanic rituals of exorcism.

In some ways, the dramaturgical account of the relationship between Italians and Muslims, encapsulated in the context of Islam in Italy, is nothing more than the dichotomous interplay made of "light and dark" characterising life abroad: from laughter to quarrel, from dinner invitations to entrance denials, from accusations of racism to acts of political correctness. These are the extreme "characters" of the people, who find themselves in the comments and responses recorded during the research, making linear and predictable relationships more difficult to envision.

Introductory Note

From this point of view, the book highlights a clearly complex and ambiguous scenario, but urges fora more balanced approach, which, though less marketable, is functional to the taking of decisions concerning private and public spheres, paving the way for more desirable, respectful, and conscious approaches to citizenship and institutional attitude.

Marco Lombardi Professor,
Department of Sociology,
Catholic University of the Sacred Heart, ITSTIME

Introduction

The day that all university students await with trepidation has finally come. On a sunny mid-June afternoon, I too am about to receive my degree. It's the day in which years of hard work are repaid. I spot my parents and my friends who have come all the way from Italy. It is a glorious day. I've made it through the end!

While I sincerely admit that I can't wait to go celebrate with friends and family (with the intent to destroy myself with lots of food), I can't help being struck by my thesis supervisor's words:

> "It's true. Today your journey at this college has come to an end. You won't be forced to study anymore. You won't have midterms and exams anymore. And you will not have to write long essays until midnight either. But, be aware. Today it might be over, but I do invite you to do the following. Ask. Challenge. Keep doing research. Appreciate the opportunity you have been given. In other words, no matter what you do, never stop being students".

Many years later, I can't be any more grateful to my professor for his simple and yet extraordinary reflection. But I do have to say, he is not 100% right. After graduation, I perhaps take his words a bit too literally and, in a blink of an eye, I obtain an MA and then I senselessly enrol in a Ph.D. programme. Or maybe my professor is right in the sense that I do not end up writing essays until midnight, but straight until 5 am on the following day. Or maybe he already knew what was going to happen...

Jokes aside, I want to reiterate it. I can't be any more obliged and enthusiastic about such words. They encourage me. They motivate me. They truly make me appreciate the great opportunity that we academics have: studying the world. I believe there is nothing more fascinating. Nothing more up to date. Nothing more stimulating. That is, there is nothing more beautiful, for all of this is a privilege. Not every person can afford to ask questions. Not everyone can doubt. Not everyone can do research. And not all of us have the chance to continue to be students.

Well aware of this, in the following years, I am captivated by politics and international security. Terrorism and radicalisation studies bewitch me. I end up as a student in the Middle East and then in the United Kingdom. But in both instances, I choose to take Italy as my case study.

I start wondering: how does Italy look like in terms of terrorism and radicalisation? Is Jihadist terrorism a spooky spectre looming over Italy too? Is the country bound to suffer its *Charlie Hebdos* and *Bataclans*?

With the intent to explore the Italian panorama, I immediately understand that such themes are complex. Terrorism and radicalisation are, indeed, not totally defined terms. They mean *different things to different people*. They are relative and often politicised concepts. And, perhaps, their essence is not ultimately understood.

In addition, it is evident that studies of Jihadist terrorism often refrain from taking into consideration a very important piece in the puzzle: the average Muslim. That's right. We frequently

INTRODUCTION

forget that terrorists do not come from nowhere, but they are from flesh and blood societies. Such Islamic communities, however, are regularly stigmatised. They are only addressed when bombs go off but are rarely the fulcra of sincere and constructive public debates.

At the beginning of this research, in fact, I do not want to talk only about terrorism and radicalisation. I also want to talk about terrorism and radicalisation. That is, I want to talk about what it means to be Muslims in today's Italy. I want to talk about racism. I want to talk about integration. I want to talk about the condition of Muslim women, second generations, and converts. I want to report joys and fears, dreams and delusions. In simpler words, I want to put the human aspect at the heart of the journey, featuring its stories, its eyes, its voice, and its essence.

Let me be clear, though. I have no unrealistic (or arrogant) aspirations. I am not entirely sure if I can do what I've just said, because, after all, it's still me, with my prejudices, faults, and ego.

Nevertheless, I still hope that this book can be a chance for dialogue and understanding. In particular, I hope that this personal journey can be an opportunity. A starting point from which people can talk about all topics, including slippery matters. To highlight differences and commonalities. To let us think. Rejoice Get angry – Criticise Build.

It's not just about terrorism. There is a whole world to discover and explore.

Yet, due to the sensitive nature of the project, I opt for the complete anonymity of every person narrated in the next chapters. Thus, all the names that appear in this journey (which takes place from north to south, visiting 15 Italian cities, from fall 2015 to end of 2017) are invented. In some cases, I even switch sites and locations, and several descriptions are intentionally vague. But, rest assured, the study's interviews, comments, and testimonies stem from real-life events and circumstances that I have personally experienced.

That specified, this book is based on 440 surveys administered inside the Italian Muslim community, which are juxtaposed to other 440 questionnaires aimed at Italian non-Muslims. Moreover, the project also features 200 interviews with Muslim participants, being the latter the main focus of the study. Despite numerous theoretical, logistical, and sociological limitations, the examined samples are still fairly representative of both the Italian Muslim and non-Muslim populations.

As we will notice in the next chapters, what emerges from the statistical analysis is, in my humble opinion, incredibly interesting. On one hand, I see and come across beautiful situations. I sense respect. Peace. Passion. Understanding. Honest hope for a better future. On the other hand, I see and come across hideous situations. I sense arrogance. Hatred. Nihilism. Close mindedness. Real worry over the country's future.

We find this type of dualism in every chapter of the book. We encounter this in chapter one, when we talk about racism, juxtaposing those who feel discriminated against to those who say they have never experienced anything bad; in the second chapter, when we look at integration, recounting both fascinating stories of inclusion and success and testimonies from people who do not want to be integrated and hate Italy; in chapter three, when we present strong women who suffer, young people who are either active or trapped between cultures, and converts who are either found peace or are

INTRODUCTION

at war with Italian society; in the fourth chapter, when we contrast those who reject violence in the name of God to others who justify and glorify it; and, finally, in the last two chapters, when Muslims and non-Muslims meet, accept and refuse each other, and discuss about the future they wish for.

All in all, this is the real essence of the book: a mixture of love and hatred, joy and sadness, light and darkness.

Remember.

This is the account of a journey, made of phrases, stories, and numbers. But *only you* are entitled to the last word.

Racism Made in Italy?

Talking about racism is difficult. That topic does not evoke good memories. Like it or not, racism is an integral part of Italian history. The infamous racial laws targeting Italian Jews during WWII are not even 100 years old. Every winter we are called to celebrate Memorial Day, that is, the discrimination, the internment, and the killing of 6 million Jews. Seeing what fear of diversity can do, schools teach us that tolerance and respect are natural antidotes to any form of hatred. And the Church constantly invites us to abide by the teachings of Jesus, made of pity, love, and hospitality.

Still, since the beginning of the humanitarian crisis in the Mediterranean, it hasn't been easy talking about history. It hasn't been easy talking about values. And it has been even more difficult putting into practice what we've been preached since our childhood. On the contrary, we've ended up politicising everything. Polarising the country. Dividing society into *racists* and *radical chic*.

Perhaps, discrimination and racism are still too fresh and slippery to ponder over. Perhaps, some historical wounds are yet to be healed. Perhaps, we are all afraid of an honest and crude dialogue on such matters. Maybe we don't really know what to do, as we learn we are afraid to look at ourselves in the mirror.

Whichever the truth, the point doesn't really change: the relationship between *new entries* and *mainstream society* is, by definition, a complicated question.

Trust me. We Italians know what we're talking about. Just ask the innumerable families moving from southern to northern Italy not long ago. Or, better, just ask those Italians who migrated to the US. Even if today's America loves Italians, we all are aware of the inhuman conditions our ancestors had to undergo in Little Italy, New York – when they were underpaid, enslaved, marginalised, and cooped up in overcrowded, abject ghettos.

I think it's no coincidence that, during my studies in California, I come across letters from workers from Veneto and Campania. Their essence is the same: although these workers contributed to the emergence of a global power, the "New World" yelled "dirty Italians" and "maccheroni" right in their face.

More than a century later, I feel we can't postpone the question any longer. The world is changing. People are moving. We cannot afford to avoid discussing racism and discrimination. Yes, even in Italy, a country with an impressive cultural history, which is becoming, day after day, increasingly diverse and multicultural.

At this point, I can't help but ask myself: what is the relationship between Italy and its citizens of foreign origin? How do the latter live in our country? What does it mean to be "foreigner" in today's Italy? And what do Italian Muslims think in this regard? Do they feel at home? Or are Moroccans, Tunisians, and Pakistanis the "new maccheroni"?

It is with this spirit that I commence my journey inside the Italian Muslim community - from East to West, from North to South, in 15 cities.

As I prepare to embark on this journey, I honestly don't expect to report many stories of racism. After all, I myself come from a family that is half Italian and half South American. We were born between Genoa and Modena. In the face of multiple difficulties, we can proudly say that we are integrated. My little cousins were born in Italy. My uncles have obtained Italian citizenship after years of hard work. My beautiful Pocahontas-alike cousins married typical Italians. During weekends, emulating *My Big Fat Greek Wedding,* we literally take over suburban Trattorias looking for delicious tortellini and lasagne. And following the Italian football team's catastrophic missed qualification to the final phase of the World Cup in Russia, we even cried our hearts out with Gigi Buffon.

In sum, despite our South American background, we are not subject to any form of discrimination. We feel accepted. We feel Italians. We can't be any happier.

But not every foreigner shares our experience.

Since the start of the voyage, it is clear that a large amount of the Muslim participants I interacted with (more than I initially expected) do not feel welcome.

I glimpse that kind of discomfort in the bottom of hundreds of eyes. And amongst these, Mohammad's eyes particularly speak to me. Owner of a bakery shop not far away from my childhood home, Mohammad came from Morocco with literally nothing. The beginning was tough, but, after much hard work, this sweet-eyed robust gentleman made it. Now, he is respected and admired by all. Love, sacrifice, quality, and entrepreneurship: Mohammad is a story of success. He's the living proof that, even in post-economic recession Italy, whoever applies his/her energies can arrive. Or at least, this is what I tell myself.

"Certainly, I have a good job and I can bring food to my table, but you just have no idea of how hard it is to be a Muslim here, Michele", Mohammad sighs.

"Why?", I ask a bit surprised.

"When I came here, I didn't speak one Italian word. I have worked day and night, humiliating myself to get where I am today. But many don't care. To these people, I'll always be a dirty Muslim, a terrorist, a backward person who mistreats women. Even if tomorrow I show up driving a red Ferrari, every Modenese's secret dream, I'd still be a 'Maruchein'. It doesn't matter what I do, for people have already decided. Even those who say they are 'open-minded' and they 'love us' because they vote left are just as racist as everyone else. That's the reality".

Stark and sober, Mohammad's words are alarming. And they are so especially because they do not remain uncorroborated. In the written questionnaires administered all over the country, the outcome is patent: 50% of the participants, that is, half of the sample (220/440), declare to feel discriminated against because of their Islamic identity.

Again, this number is startling. While I'm probably not able to fully process Mohammad's emotions, I like to think that I might have slightly more empathy towards migrants. You know, those who escape war and misery, arrive on a boat from Libya, do not speak Italian, do not have a job, and do not know their life's trajectory. In my biased mind, that makes more sense, doesn't it? But stories like Mohammad's leave me puzzled. I can't help questioning why a person like him, who's been here for a while, has a *good* job, and seems *so* integrated, feels this way.

Why do 50% of Italian Muslims say they feel discriminated against? What's going on?

With many questions in mind, I begin my interviews by asking participants how they feel to be Muslims in today's Italy. And, like in the surveys, I encounter stories of racism, discrimination, and Islamophobia.

Even though it has been associated to non-observant Muslims, the term "Islamophobia" is almost intrinsic to the narrative that juxtaposes "Islam" and the "West". According to many interviewees from all over, it's exactly this fear of Islam that allows and justifies the stigmatisation of the Italian Muslim community.

"Italy is a xenophobic and Islamophobic country", sentences a worker in Milan. "Once, an old lady was forced to sit close to me because the bus was packed; in the end, she did seat down, but she looked at me as if I were a leper just because my beard is bit longer than normal and my skin is darker than everyone else's", recounts outraged Hassan from Bergamo. "It's natural that we experience racism and that society discriminates us because", reveals a Moroccan university student in Rome, for "people don't know us, hear lots of fake stories, make up ideas of Muslims and Islam that are completely detached from reality, and… game over". To a Senegalese young adult from Naples, Italy's fear of Islam would even be inevitable because, "more or less, every person is racist and, thus, so are you". To such respect, one Gambian citizen living in Verona asks me the following: "In your opinion, how can I believe that there is no racism when I am a foreigner, I don't eat pork, I don't drink wine, I'm Muslim, and, above all, I'm a black Muslim?".

That asserted, according to 25% of the interviewees (48/200), such racism and Islamophobia would be products of two factors: terrorism and loss of identity. As we are going to see in the second last chapter, 7 out of 10 non-Muslim Italians are afraid that attacks like the ones that hit Paris, Brussels, and London might occur in Italy too. Palpable in panicky post-*Charlie Hebdos* filled concrete blocks and armed forces guarding plazas and monuments, the terrorist spectre is what numerous Muslims deem responsible for society's racism.

I was able to witness this claim in Florence when, on the same day, Jihadist terrorists attack Brussels' underground. Doing research, I run into a small group of devotees on their way to the city's Islamic centre. Walking alongside the Cathedral and Giotto's bell tower, we start chatting about their overall condition as Muslims, when one man informs everyone that Brussels had just been stricken. "Are there casualties? How many?", asks a terrified Ahmet.

I am not exaggerating. I can see horror, distress, and helplessness down to his soul.

"Now it's going to be hard, as usual in these cases, to walk around in the street; every time these bastards commit atrocities and dishonour Islam, we are the ones suffering the consequences", says Ahmet's fuming friend Abdul. "My wife", continues Abdul, "wears the veal: she already feels like everyone is looking at her, assuming that she gets beaten up... and now she'll have to face comments by stupid kids on the bus yelling her 'terrorist'. And I will have to watch, listen to all that crap, and do nothing. Does this seem fair to you?".

One week later, Abdelkair tells me that, in Torpignattara, Rome, racism "gets under the skin". "I know, I am weird, but just because I come from the Arab world, it doesn't mean that I am a terrorist; okay, I am ugly too, but I am harmless and very nice", amusingly reassures Abdelkair. And so does Aruk, owner of a Kebab shop in Bologna as he treats me to a "Ke-BOMB-one" against "Islamophobia and raging anxiety in the city".

According to others, fear of terrorism has little to do with racist attitudes. On the contrary, for these people, it's all about identity, for Italian culture feels threatened by Islamic presence. To begin with, as I hear in Padua, Varese, and Venice, there would be an inherent rejection of Islam by Catholics. "Many Italians just can't accept that there are foreigners and, God forbid, Italian Muslims", or that "a mosque could be built next to the Vatican", or that "people are coming back to Islam and many churches lose followers".

"Islam", as explained by an Islamic devotee in Cantù, close to Lake Como, "goes against the Catholic status quo and, as a result, we are not always welcome". "Are you really staggered by the existence of racism and Islamophobia?", asks a Somalian in Centocelle, Rome. "In your opinion", teases the latter, "can wider society accept a religion other than Catholicism and, for the love of God, a Muslim Italian?".

According to Ish, a 38-year-old Moroccan who sells vegetables next to the Mole Antonelliana in Turin, the whole matter is not strictly a religious one. In reality, it's all about the loss of traditions and habits, particularly by the current youth.

"Michele, I've been living here for many years and I can see how Italian society has been changing", tells Ish.

"In which ways do you think society is changing?", I ask him.

"I see a great loss of traditional values. People don't go to Church anymore, they don't know what to do anymore, who to follow, what to think. Then they look at us and feel scared".

"Why would they feel scared?", I inquire.

"Maybe because they are not accustomed to certain values anymore, feel threatened by new ones, and become racist. You see, today youngsters, and adults too, want to do everything. They take everything for granted, they think the world is theirs, and that there are no rules…again, people think they are allowed to do whatever they wish, whenever they wish. The type of racism targeting us is nothing but the reaction to more women wearing the veil, more Halal meet shops, and more people fasting during Ramadan. In a wrong way, many young Italians come to believe that all these things are a menace, for they feel judged and are afraid that they will have to change their lifestyles. But it's not so".

Unfortunately, we are not fully able to determine the factors that really fuel the kind of racism we hear about – might they be related to fear of terrorism or might they be linked to loss of cultural and religious identity.

What is noticeable is, instead, the sense of disparity and inequality. In truth, many feel treated "differently" because they are perceived as "different". And this feeling pervades multiple facets of daily life. For instance, 40% of the surveyed participants (175/440) admit they struggle at finding a house because Italians won't rent places to foreigners. "They said it right into my face, 'Here we don't rent places to people like you'", recounts an incandescent Amre in Turin's outskirt.

Souleyman's testimony doesn't differ much: "We're Muslims, we come from Mali, we're black, and my wife and daughters wear the veil; who knows what people think as we search for a small apartment as we come always back empty handed; I know damn well that we'll end up asking our communities for help, for those I interact with don't want us to live here in Brescia".

It's not over yet. Even when one does find a house, mingling with society can also be a tricky process. More than 3 out of 10 examined subjects (150/440) believe that they Islamic identity does not help their blending at school, for that latter is not always acknowledged and accepted. Amongst multiple stories muddied by mockery and embarrassment, the one by Miriam from Reggio Calabria is particularly sad. One day, her middle school teacher hangs her coat on her head telling her that "thing", meaning the veil, makes her look like a "coat hanger", making Miriam "blush in shame".

Even once out of school things do not always improve. Although we will grant Muslim women a voice in two chapters, men too can be affected by how they dress, specially at the workplace. Kidding around, a Pakistani employee from Arcella, Padua, reckons to be "really lucky to have a job because [this] long beard is worth 6-7 unsuccessful interviews". "This is the reason why I work for other Muslim immigrants", confides Albiel in Milan. "My name", he continues, "and my appearance are too Arab to appease old, grumpy clients from this area and, even if I do try to speak with a Milanese accent and act more Western, they always find an excuse to leave me at home".

Being personally familiar with the university domain, Amal's work-related difficulties make me reflect too. A recent engineer graduate, Amal struggles at finding occupation. "I'm aware that it's hard for everyone out there…I know the market is competitive and saturated. But I've been one of the best students of my programme and when I see people who haven't studied as much as I have and whose results haven't been as good as mine, well, I wonder why I bothered to go to university in the first place. Then, I realise that, maybe, foreigners are okay, and they can work in Italy, but as long as they do those humble jobs that no one wants to do anymore".

Whilst the great majority of the sample is not unemployed, 39% (170/440) still affirm they encounter difficulties at work on account of being Muslim. To such regard, a conversation with a group of North African workers close to Reggio Emilia is particularly noteworthy:

"Guys, what do you mean when you say that you feel discriminated against at work on account of being Muslim?", I start investigating.

"Look, I think I can speak for all of us", replies Ahmed in a resolute manner. "It's not like our bosses and colleagues single us out openly…they can't really do that. They do that in a subtle way, through funny looks and small pranks. Sometimes they say blasphemies, even if they don't even believe in God, just because they know that bothers me. And, just like children, they do that repeatedly to see if I lose my temper. I tried not to let them get to me, but it's hard. Even during lunch breaks, things don't get any easier. Not eating prosciutto and not drinking wine in this region of the country is no simple task. I frequently hear people laughing behind my back or I glance them staring as if I were an alien….not to mention during Ramadan, when colleagues intentionally provoke me by repeatedly asking if I'm tired, again, just to get on my nerves. In all of this, I can recognise their tacit sense of arrogance and superiority".

Another truly controversial matter is the inability to find appropriate places of worship. Indeed, 56% of surveyed subjects (245/440) confirm they have issues at finding a proper mosque. And so do numerous interviewees, for in cities such as Milan, Brescia, and Bergamo, the question of the mosque is highly divisive. "There's nothing to do", moans Sara just outside a tiny cultural centre in Bergamo. "We've tried everything, including concrete plans of actions and steady projects. We've found the money, we've guaranteed the use of Italian language in sermons, and we've invited municipal and regional authorities to supervise the project step after step. The result? We're still here, almost in the middle of the street. If this isn't discrimination, I don't know what it is".

"Let me be clear; things aren't so bad here in Brescia", yields a Kosovar follower at a local mosque. "But we're starting to be many and the space isn't enough anymore. We've always behaved properly, we pay taxes, and many of us are Italian and/or have Italian citizenship: why don't they give us the permits to build a new mosque? I don't really see the problem". Fatima's words inside a bakery in Milan might be even more eloquent. "The greatest manifestation of discrimination, the biggest offense", says the women while holding my hand, "is the question of the mosque: as long as we pray in garages and basements, there is absolutely no problem, but when we ask for what is already granted by the Italian Constitution, no thanks!". "There will never be a proper mosque and we will never be equal to the Italians until the media carry out their crusade against our communities", echoes a Tunisian customer.

To such regard, it's the very relationship with the Italian media to fuel the most controversial sentiments within the Muslim population. According to 82% of the surveyed participants (358/440), there is a media war against Islam and Muslims. Unsurprisingly, when it comes to the media, even the most composed can't help being highly critical and suspicious. In fact, the first question that I get usually asked is: "Excuse me sir, are you a journalist?".

When people learn that I am a simple researcher, I notice they look more relaxed and act more supportive. Subsequent smiles and good vibes make me hypothesise, yet, that a positive answer might actually entice less propensity to participate in my study. But luckily, this is not the case and, as interlocutors feel more comfortable voicing their opinions, many share their thoughts about Italian media: "The media are the cancer of this country", "We are at war with newspapers", "The media and the journalists are worse than the terrorists", "The media are the bastards", "The media are serving the world's strong powers against Islam", and "TV and the press are the number one enemy for every Muslim in the world".

Worth of mention is the tête-à-tête with an Egyptian butcher in the Roman suburbs:

"Why wouldn't you like Italian press when they deal with the Islamic matter?", I ask.

"What? Don't you see? Don't you see they don't care about the accuracy of events? These people know nothing about Islam and Muslims. Only when something bad happens, let's say a terrorist attack, the wider public takes an interest and want to learn a bit more. But even in such cases, no one comes and asks us directly. The media take care of everything".

"What do you mean when you say that the media take care of everything?".

"They make stuff up".

"Excuse me, which stuff?".

"I once saw a very notorious journalist from a famous TV show here in the area. I saw him looking and paying young Arabs to say radical things and prove that the situation is critical. He did this to obtain, of course, more attention and audience".

"These are really serious claims. Are you sure it was him? Maybe you've mistaken him for someone else".

"I'm not stupid. Even if I'm a butcher, I know what I saw, I swear on Mohammad, peace upon Him".

Although the veracity of such allegations can't be really verified, the message is clear: to the overwhelmingly majority of the study's participants, their relationship with Italian media is utterly complicated. And it looks like it won't improve any time soon, because "until this climate of uncertainty persists, we'll always be walking to the slaughterhouse", states Alessandro, an Italian convert from Marche.

With the intent to intellectually provoke conversers, at this state I often ask why the media should be against Italian Muslims. After all, what's in it for TV shows and newspapers? Couldn't they just focus on Juventus, Inter, and José Mourinho's bold acts?

Jokes aside, according to 8 out 10 interviewees (160/200) there are two reasons that justify racism and Islamophobia in the media. The first is merely economic.

One couple I bump into in front of Milan's football stadium backs up this theory: "The more rubbish you talk about us and Islam, the more newspapers you sell". In a keen attempt to illustrate such claims, Bimo, a journalism student, puts it this way: "Michele, it's all about the audience; you notice that people want to read about terrorism, the chief-editor makes rational calculations, tells you how much you are to write about that attack and what you are to write about that terrorist; as a journalist, you obey and you sensationalise your story as much as you can. The more you do this, the more money your newspaper earns, and the more status you acquire". "As a matter of fact, the media could pay us a little…we can send them our IBANs if they want, taking that we are a money-making machine for them", ironically states Ibrahim in Monza.

In addition to selling newspapers, there would also be a substantial political motivation behind Islamophobia in the media. Eating a succulent spicy chicken platter in the centre of Milan, a proud and corpulent 60-year-old man from Libya unravels the riddle:

"We all know that televisions and newspapers all have clear political orientations. This is no secret. If you create a common enemy and instil fear, you get votes. Certainty, there are more pressing issues, such as the economy and corruption. But if you manage to distract public opinion, craft cases that don't even exist, and misuse isolated acts by a few creeps, while you keep building an electoral campaign against immigrants and people of different colour, it's a big leap towards a seat in Parliament".

To Genoese Mahmut, the spectrum would be even wider, though: "The media war does not affect Italy, but the whole world too. The West is experiencing an almost unprecedented political crisis, just look at how the European Union has managed the Greek and the migration emergencies. As Islam is a fast-growing religion, there's a clear message that we are to be kept under control, from Italy to Sweden". Along the same lines, a Syrian-Italian doctor close to Trento also refers to this type of intended political control: "If you inject anxiety into the public, you can justify racism and, with it, the control of both people and, most importantly, ideas. In this sense, the relationship between media and the population in recent times, made of uncertainty, slogans, and falsities, is deeply and intimately symbiotic".

If we were to take only the above mentioned comments and testimonies, we'd have no escape. In the reported stories, our country appears detached and insensitive. According to these participants, it looks like Italy discriminates and acts racist vis-à-vis its Muslim citizens.

Genuine and trustworthy, such stories however, only partly embody the overall Muslim experience in Italy. Luckily, my journey also features men and women who have never faced any type of racism or discrimination. And even though they are a minority, these people still make up for the 45% of the survey (198/440). "Italy is not a racist country, for it's full of good people", reassures a worker from Bangladesh in Rome, because, in the end, "Italians are like us... they don't discriminate against other brothers", echoes a Jordanian craftsman.

"You Italians", articulates Abbas in Venice, "have travelled and experienced the same things that we live today; it's for this reason that you guys understand us and treat us nicely". In Rome, a Palestinian young man explains how his refugee status interestingly helps him avoid racisms: "Maybe people have been nice to me because I've been kicked out of my land or maybe they pity me, I don't know. The point being, since I've arrived, the Romans have become my friends and I've been given much assistance and respect".

Home to almost 30% of Italian Muslims, Lombardy too displays bits of normality, respect, and solidarity. "I've been told that Milan and its inhabitants were racist; as far as I'm concerned, I've never encountered a single racist person, for I've always felt at home", reveals a Moroccan student. "I always hear talks about racism and discrimination on TV and in the press, but we've never had one problem here in Brescia; nobody has ever mistreated us, we've always been free to walk into any store, and we've taken our children to the park without anyone staring at us", enumerates Dedo, a Bosnian labourer. Similarly, Rashida from Catania recalls how at school, "no one, even inside the classroom, has ever been bothered by the fact I wear the veil; on the contrary, it has been an opportunity for dialogue and understanding with my Italian friends".

Aisha's memory of her first days in Milan as a refugee is simply touching:

"I had recently arrived and, as such, I had no diapers for my little daughter. Actually, I had nothing and I could only speak a few English words. I went out for a walk and I wanted to cry. I was desperate. One guy – I think he worked in a nearby bar - saw me and asked me what was wrong. I didn't really understand much of what he was saying, but I could definitely see that he was genuinely trying to help. I started gesticulating and made him understand that I needed diapers. The guy asked me to wait. He returned a bit later with diapers for me - for me, a perfect stranger. I started crying and I hugged him".

I have to be honest. I too am really moved by Aisha's story. If episodes of racism and discrimination sadden me, acts of humanity beyond every label fill my heart with joy. And I am lucky enough to recreate such positive feelings following a conversation with a group of Senegalese young adults behind the Garibaldi train station in Naples:

"Guys, as Muslims, do you feel discriminated against?", I ask in a warm springtime afternoon.

"Are you crazy?", they reply all together.

"Not the case? Is everything good?".

"What could be wrong? We have everything here. We've escaped famine and misery, and we're happy to be in Naples", excitedly states the youngest of the group.

"Are you aware that many people, amongst whom I believe there are numerous Neapolitans, would not be so happy to live in Naples?".

"Their loss. They don't know what they are missing. People from Naples are fantastic and crack us up!".

"Do they treat you nice?".

"They have seen we're good boys. When they can, they help out and even give us pizza".

"Here people smile at us and love us", mouths another man.

"Do you know why?", starts over the youngest. "Because these people don't see us differently. These people, like us, grapple. These people, like us, have left home before, have felt lonely, and have been treated poorly. These people understand what we're going through and, at times, all it takes is a smile, especially from a beautiful girl, to make you feel at home, even if your family is still in Africa. These people can't discriminate against us, because, if they do it, they go against their nature, which is sensitive and hospitable".

"In fact,", continues another young man, "Neapolitans know what racism is and, thus, try to make us feel part of the city. We tease each other, we laugh, we kid around, we also get mad at each other, but they all love us. Imagine that when Naples wins a big match or our compatriot Koulibaly scores a goal, some business owners give us free food and drinks to celebrate".

Interviewees who had previously lived abroad also debunk claims that Italy is a racist nation. Maybe a bit surprisingly, not only do these individuals speak highly of our country, but they also hold that Italy is less racist than other realities. In the words of a Moroccan family guy weighing his experience in France and Turin: "One can't think that there is racism in Italy. I've lived in France too and that's where you have discrimination, because you got to think French, eat French, speak French, but work as an underpaid Moroccan or Algerian".

Analogously, an Albanian citizen recounts his precedent in Austria with sorrow: "I was living in Vienna, but Austrians are cold and, you can say, they look down on you, especially when they understand you're Muslim. I love it here in Venice, for I work a lot and people respect me for it". Remembering Switzerland, Muhammad maintains that, "Swiss people are truly closeminded and racist; I've been there for ten months and, although I speak French, no one, but really no one, has even spoken to me. Here it's 100 times better, for Italians make me feel one of them".

Furthermore, practically and professionally speaking, not everyone believes that racist and Islamophobic attitudes automatically affect every sphere of daily. In actuality, most sampled individuals confirm they do not experience any harshness at the workplace (221/440, that is 50%). In terms of employment, this picture seems to be corroborated by the fact that only 8% of the questionnaires' participants (36/440) are unemployed. "There are job opportunities in Italy, indeed; maybe they are not remunerated much, but at least we can work", observes an Indonesian worker in Gallarate. As one of his Nigerian friends reiterates: "I don't really get those brothers who claim that there are no jobs here; in my opinion, there are plenty of occupations and, provided that you demonstrate that you want to do stuff, sooner or later they will hire you".

To such regard, I am positively impressed by the degree of respect enjoyed by certain ethnic groups within the larger Muslim community. Sadly, the vile aggressions against Bangladeshi waiters in Rome are still vivid in the nation's memory. But as I stroll around our capital, I notice that workers from Bangladesh – who have arrived in great numbers in the last 10 years - are widely respected and highly requested by bars and restaurants in the town centre. "They are like work-machines and, even if the sky fell down, they would always find a job", says (with a hit of envy) an Iraqi asylum seeker in Torpignattara, Rome. "That's because the 'Bangla' are serious and rigorous people, and that's why everybody wants them", admires Moroccan Anas.

Further, as far as employers and colleagues are concerned, in about 60% of the times (119/200), interviewees declare they do not suffer any hardship at their workplace. Not far away from the bakery in which Mohammed told me the story about the red Ferrari, a group of Turkish workers contend that "Italy is a country made of people who go beyond appearances. We work in a local factory. We've been here for 20 years and our colleagues have never caused us any trouble, they've never looked at us funnily, and they've never disrespected us". In a similar fashion, Abderrabak, a small firm employee from Padua's province, puts it this way: "People from the Veneto region are a bit closeminded and, at the beginning, it's not easy to gain their respect; but as long as you show that you want to work and that you're a straightforward person, they will let you be and you can work really well".

Perhaps, this is exactly the point: the most important thing is the type of honesty and respect each person proves to possess. Besides, it's fair to say that not everyone cares about the next person's religious creed: "Provided that you work and that you stay in your place, people don't really care about who you are and what you believe in", states Ayman in Sampierdarena, Genoa.

Moreover, about 40% of the surveyed participants (166/440) admit they have no issues at finding appropriate places of worship. Although they are the minority and they do concede that bigger mosques would be much appreciated, the latter are nevertheless satisfied with what they already have. Throughout my journey, I often find myself enthralled by how people manage to restructure and reuse ridiculously narrow and, frankly, shabby sites. For instance, I see Imams and followers crawl, climb, and "fade away" in a maze of bone chilling, dark basements and hidden rooms that can compete with the Tower of London.

Let's be honest. Several locations might not possess every legal permit and might not be that pretty either, but 4 out of 10 interviewees (80/200) don't mind. "In Bangladesh, we got nothing, whereas here in Rome we have a building where we can pray", happily explains a Roman Imam. "I don't agree with certain brethren", complains a devotee in Verona. "When they accuse Italy of discriminating against us because they don't let us build bigger mosques, I don't think that is fair; we already have our sites, nobody says anything to us, and we're fine. We can be ourselves, and this is a great bliss". "If we can build larger ones, that is great, but let's take a look around; how many mosques and cultural centres can you see? I would say that, after all, this is a sign that things aren't going so bad in this country", asserts an Imam in Catania.

In addition to the question of the mosque, not every person approves of the established tense relationship between the media and the larger community. Whilst surveys overwhelmingly show that Muslims feel the media are at war with Islam, in almost half of the interviews (96/200), a reflective voice challenges the dominant narrative. According to the latter, disinformation and Islamophobia would not be the product of rationally orchestrated scheme against Islam. They might not be linked to ratings, money, and politics. Rather, they might be product of great ignorance.

To this respect, Fadi's comments are thought-provoking:

"I don't think we can say that there's racism in Italy. Even though we like demonising them, the media are not really racist either. At the bottom of their disinformation, however, there is much ignorance, which then fuels everything".

"What do you mean, precisely?", I ask.

"Italian society doesn't know much about Islam. But this is natural, for we haven't always been here, and people do not always have the chance to meet and get to know Muslims. Like them, those who work in news agencies also know little of Islam. But society still needs news, for the show must go on and, hence, you end up talking about things you don't fully understand. At this point, what can we really say to Italians who watch TV and read newspapers and ultimately get scared? It's not racism, it's ignorance".

Whether or not it is about this type of unfamiliarity, there are probably other ways to bridge the gap. Among all the considerations I listen to, two particular ones catch my attention. The first comes from another Egyptian butcher in Milan: "My dear, it's not a matter of discrimination; media are the same everywhere, they've always been like that... even when I was in Egypt, they used to talk trash about Israel, the United States, and Europe. Here it is kind of the same and we should not get so worked up about it, for the media do not really represent Italy, or any country for that matter".

Why do you think the butcher's reasoning intrigues me? Because I think he offers a different approach. It might be the nature of the job that, in this case, allows for racist and Islamophobic tones in the media, but, being cognizant of that, one must not care too much. For one cannot judge a nation based on what he/she hears and watches on TV.

This perfectly connects to the second consideration by a Moroccan university student from Bologna. "The media write and say bad things about us?", asks Fatma. "We just must not care. Let's behave well, let actions talk for us, and let journalists write whatever they want. Let's show these people they have no reason to write rubbish about us. But if instead we take offense after every piece of nonsense they write and show, if people see that we get mad, and if we end up making a mess, we actually end up validating those who attack us. And that's when people are really going to start discriminating against us, because they will see in us what they read and watch. Therefore, the choice is only ours".

Fatma's words are ever so powerful. They shift the balance of the whole matter by introducing visions of sensitivity, strategy, and intelligence. In other terms, Fatma tells us that the media are important *if and only if* people allow it. Hence, one must not get angry, because good deeds and actions count more than thousands of words and images. And in the end, people, with their intelligence and sensitivity, decide which path they want to follow.

All in all, what does emerge from this whole picture? What do Italian Muslims think in terms of racism and discrimination?

Numbers and interviews indicate that the community might be split in two.

On one side lies a bloc that feels highly discriminated against. It perceives and touches the type of racism made in Italy. It feels marginalised due to its Islamic identity. It is impacted by criminal actions that, as we are going to see shortly, are widely and expressly condemned by the community. It is accused of undermining Italian culture and folklore. It is still part of society but does feel betrayed when it comes to the matter of the mosque. It feels out of place, both at work and at school. It feels demonised by the media each day for money, electoral purposes, and geopolitical dynamics. In the end, this group feels humiliated and exploited. Hurt, frustrated, and discouraged, it has to face a country deemed racist. For this bloc, discrimination and Islamophobia are real. For this bloc, daring to be Muslim is a fundamentally problematic aspect.

Diametrically opposite stands the other bloc. Unlike its counterpart, this group does not feel discriminated against. Not at all. It perceives and touches the type of hospitality made in Italy. It is unable to sense and experience the kind of racism it hears about. It is not overshadowed by Jihadist terrorism, nor by the interaction with Italian culture. Its Muslim identity does not seem to collide with the various facets of daily life. It features no difficulties at the workplace or at school. It doesn't feel betrayed by the system, for its members can pray freely. And it doesn't even care much about the media, for it believes that the latter can't fully represent an entire nation. After all, to this group, racism, discrimination, and Islamophobia remain distant.

Perhaps, it is this kind of dualism that, from an external perspective, fascinates me. Is there racism and discrimination against Italian Muslims? It depends on the people you decide to ask this query. It's like a Picasso's painting – a bit confusing, but incomparably penetrant. Probably, the truth hides *where* you decide to look.

A Matter of Integration

Many of us, for one reason or another, are familiar with the word "integration". We often hear this term when talking about modern Italian-Americans - especially when they are offered prestigious positions. Probably, we hear this word after terrorist attacks perpetrated by jihadists born and raised in the targeted nation. Many of us recognise this word on the news and in footages showing increasingly multi-ethnic schools and neighbourhoods. And finally, I am quite sure that many of us hear discussions over integration within the current debate on immigration and security.

Although the above-mentioned situations do differ, their common thread is, in some way, the benign nature of this constant called "integration". Good integration is the reason for societal achievements by Italian-Americans. Good integration can counteract homegrown terrorism - more integration means less resentment towards society, many believe. Good integration can facilitate the social and professional advancement of foreign citizens in increasingly multicultural realities. Likewise, we consider integration as an indispensable tool to tackle controversial issues such as immigration and security - greater integration can create more open, cohesive and secure societies.

In essence, integration is something advantageous, virtuous and, therefore, desirable.

However, despite undisputed beneficial properties, I can't help but ask myself the following: what does "integration" mean? How is "integration" recognised and how does it manifest itself? And, above all, who decides who is "integrated" and who is not?

It is important to ask these questions. Firstly, because the concept of integration itself is relative. It is subject to the historical and social interaction between societies and specific groups - in our case, Muslims in Italy. And integration can also be a subjective concept, since it depends on who the main actor is. Secondly, the degree of integration of an individual is difficult to measure impartially, since integration is a personal matter, after all.

Therefore, I would like to make two clarifications. First, this chapter only explores the dynamics of integration between Italian Muslims and their society. For now, we will not dedicate much time to an equally important aspect, that is, non-Muslim Italians' opinions on integration. Second, recognising the relative nature of the concept in question, for the sake of analysis, it is considered as "integration" the conciliation, devoid of existential conflicts, between Islamic identity and Italian society.

That asserted, this is the question we are all waiting for: after all, are Muslims in Italy integrated or are they not?

If by "integration" we mean the existence of people who reconcile their Muslim identity with Italian society, finding those commonalities that make life in Italy happy (or at least without serious existential issues), then, on the one hand, yes, many are integrated.

The interviews, in this case more than the surveys, offer many insights in this regard. To begin with, more than 50% of the interviewees (123/200) show how their Islamic identity can espouse certain fundamental values of Italian society, such as sense of family and hospitality.

As a matter of fact, an elderly Libyan gentleman laughs a bit under his moustache when I ask him if there are any big differences between Muslims in Italy and society. "Us and the Italians are family people; we like to spend many hours at the table with relatives and friends; we like to share the joys and sorrows and everyone knows everything about everyone; I believe that you and us have much more in common than you and the Germans or you and the English". "Come and sit with us", a Moroccan restaurateur gently invites me inside his crowded restaurant in Segrate. "Eat and stay with us, for we are all part of a big family, as if it were Christmas or New Year; as for you, the guest is always welcome and, when you want to come, you are always welcome". "All those we know just love Italy, because culture, ways of doing things, the importance of the family, and even the people are so similar to the way we grew up with in our countries of origin", says a Kuwaiti cleric south of Milan.

It is not too surprising that others share stories of friendship, love, and esteem for non-Muslim Italians. "I have so many Italian friends, Catholics and others, and we love each other," proudly says Amhedin Modena. Omar, from Mali, also claims to have "met so many extraordinary people in Bergamo who love me, even though I am Muslim; indeed, perhaps we love each other more than our biological brothers". "I got married to an Italian Catholic woman and it was the best thing in my life", recalls a romantic Taysir in the centre of Genoa. "I respect the Italians because, unlike other people, they also think of us; maybe at the beginning you struggle, but when you make friends, like me, then it's like becoming part of a big family, which is always there for you when you have bad moments", concludes Samir in Palermo.

Another attractive aspect is the Italian way of life. "I love doing things with my friends," says Medina with enthusiasm. As does Sarah: "As a woman, I love Italy; it is the country of fashion, perfumes and good music and every time sales are on, my sisters and I buy a bag of stuff and we are always trendy". "Whenever I can, I always try to go to the stadium and I watch all the games on television because I am a football fan and I can't do without it, "admits Said, an AC Milan supporter.

Worthy of notice is my conversation with an Egyptian who goes by the (very) Italian name Mimmo:

"Why do you have people call you 'Mimmo'?", I asked him amusedly.

"One, it's easier to pronounce it than my real name. Two, when I arrived, I met this person called Mimmo and I wanted to be like him: he was always in the little square with friends, having a drink, he was always well dressed, he talked a thousand times on the phone with his mother, he was a lover of good food and I saw him get slapped more than once at the disco… I thought that if I called myself Mimmo, maybe that would bring me luck and I would live like him".

"Wait, including getting slapped?".

"Especially for the slaps!".

"Really? Why?".

"Because he always got slapped by pretty girls. If that's the price to pay, I'm in! But I will be luckier".

A Matter of Integration

If these testimonies indicate how Islamic identity can be reconciled and find its space within society, then it is not surprising that many individuals declare that they love our country. In the surveys, these amount to 81% of the sample (351/440), claiming to love Italy and its culture, showing their desire to be part of it.

In the interviews, once again, more than half of the participants (around 130/200) share their affection for our nation. "I love this country, I love everything about Italy, from music to pizza, from soccer to women", declares a Tajiki citizen in Florence. According to a Roman Bangladeshi vendour, "Italy is the most beautiful country in the world and we are so fortunate to live here". "Not only do I owe my happiness to Italy," a Tunisian salesman in Brescia exclaims excited. "If I had remained at home, I would be in prison by now, and they would have tortured my family and, most likely, I would have died. Thank you, Italy, because you gave me my life again". "No, really, I can only thank Italy and Italians, for they welcomed me, gave me a job, and allowed me to build my happiness and, above all, the happiness of my husband and my daughter ", reiterates an Iraqi woman in Bergamo.

That's true. Love does not necessarily equal to integration. You can love a nation and still not share values and culture – just like it is possible to nurture feelings of affection without finding commonalities between Islamic identity and Italian society. However, it is also fair to state that the kind of love and gratitude towards Italy often represents a starting point for those who proudly defined themselves as "integrated" subjects.

"How can I not be integrated, given that I love this nation madly?", asks Fawas, from Tunisia, in Como. "We love Italy and we cannot help but integrate with the magnificent culture of this place", explains Ghazi in Rome. "Us Shiites too adore Italy", Alì reveals in Reggio Emilia's countryside, for "we are grateful to the Italians for allowing our integration to take place, and this is the reason why we love Italy as much as Lebanon and Iran".

Therefore, it may not be a coincidence that dozens of respondents say they feel Italian. Considering that 60% (254/440) have been residing in Italy for more than 5 years, dozens of interlocutors speak with Lombard, Venetian, Roman, and Sicilian accents! To the point that I often come across typically regional colourful expressions such as "Maremma m ...", "Ma li m ... tua", "Belin" and, alarmingly, "Bella zio!".

But in all seriousness, what strikes me is the true, passionate desire to feel Italian by both those who arrived and those who were here.

"I feel Italian, period", sentences an Albanian gentleman in his fifties. As does Sahir, thirty, from Milan: "Yes, I was born in Morocco, but I have always been here. I grew up watching Bim Bum and Bam with Kinder Cereali; I feel Italian and I do all the things Italians do, even if I observe Ramadan. I have nothing to do with people living in Morocco". "I dream of becoming Italian one day because I want to be Italian and I want my children to be Italian", prays a Bangladeshi waiter in Padua. I also find very touching what Hamsa, from Egypt, wishes for himself: "When Allah calls me and my days end, if I can ask for this, I would like to die here, in this country, amongst my Italian friends and I want to be buried at the municipal cemetery next to my Italian friends who are already there".

A Matter of Integration

At this point, I believe the time has come to share the story of Kamal, not only due to its essence, but also because it encapsulates all the dynamics we have encountered so far.

Shy and somewhat introverted, Kamal doesn't always look at me in the eye. If I didn't know any better, I would think he seems almost embarrassed to tell me about his extraordinary journey. Perhaps it's because that simple-mannered man really conceals a story of dedication and sacrifice. Born in Algeria and moving to Turin as a new-born, Kamal's childhood is not easy. His father, a low paid worker, cannot afford to pay for his son's school bus. Sun, snow and rain... the boy always walks for miles. When at school, Kamal cannot afford to eat at the school cafeteria, and his clothes are constantly out of fashion. Yet, he never feels an outcast. No, he feels part of its class, its school, and its city, which is Turin. Finally, he is one of the best students graduating. Now, he studies for the medicine admission exam. He dreams of finding a cure for cancer, but he also makes pizzas to help his father and his two little sisters to study. In his free time, Kamal runs and is in great shape! He wants to learn how to cook traditional local dishes too, because, as he admits, he's crazy about "Agnolotti del Plin". Simply put, Kamal's a stud.

"You've come a long way," I say from behind the counter of the pizzeria he works at.

"I'm lucky".

"Are you happy?".

"I couldn't ask for more. I study and I make pizzas".

"Don't you wish for anything more from life sometimes?".

"Sure, everyone does. But I've already won".

"What do you mean?".

"I can do things that my parents couldn't do. I can study, work, play and have fun. In Algeria, this wouldn't have been possible".

"How do you describe your life as an Algerian Muslim from Turin?".

"As you said: as an Algerian Muslim from Turin".

"What do you feel most?".

"It's easy, I am from Turin. Yes, I was born in Algeria, I am Muslim and I bring with me the beautiful things of that culture. But I grew up here. This is my home. I studied here. My first love was Elisa. I support Juventus and, when I can, I go to the stadium. Even if someone says that I am not a real Italian, it does not matter, for I feel Italian, I live like an Italian, I am proud to be Italian. And I have the duty to give something back to my country and to all those who believe in me.".

"Is it a problem to reconcile your Muslim identity with Italian customs?".

"Never been. I am grateful to this country and I love it. I bring the best from of my culture and I take the best from yours. I have never had any problems making friends, being respected, and integrating. This is me".

Unfortunately, not everyone can boast Kamal's strength, nor can all cling to his sense of belonging to Italian society while remaining proudly Muslim. Perhaps exceptional, Kamal's story is a hymn to integration, a true union between Islamic identity and Italian society. Because, to Kamal, as for the subjects mentioned so far, integration is real and is about one's identity. A combined Muslim and Italian identity. Which loves and adopts the Italian customs. Which loves

Italians. Which is in love with Italy. Which, with an open heart, declares to be part of the country. In other words, one which lives Italy.

However, if on the one hand we meet the various Mimmos and the various Kamals, on the other hand I run into worrying narratives. Narratives of closure and rejection, which discourage an already intricate process of integration. Narratives that do not intend to reconcile Islamic identity and Italian society, internalising the "good" from both sides. Narratives that, unfortunately, are incompatible with the values and lives of most of the population.

Although the vast majority of the sample says to love Italy, polls indicate that almost 20% (85/440) would abolish school Christmas plays out of respect for Islam. 41% (179/440) would not welcome their children's adoption of "Western" habits and customs. 39% (170/440) would not support marriages with non-Muslim Italians. And 44% (192/440) wishes for the establishment of a Mufti, an Islamic court, to which refer to instead of the Italian State.

While these statistics could also be contextualised and interpreted in different ways, the interviews leave me with little doubts. Unfortunately, within the community, there are subjects whose opinions on Italy and its culture conceal hatred.

The Christian faith, deemed false and inferior, is immediately targeted: "The Christian religion is a great lie and anyone who celebrates Christmas and Easter goes to hell", thunders Anas in Milan. And in Rome, Mahdi, from Saudi Arabia, mocks me as follows: "Do you want to do a research on Islam? Take the Koran, learn that the only religion is Islam and then I invite you to the bar". "The priests are all sexually frustrated, and, if they knew about Islam, they would not be pedophiles and helpless, having lots of children", says one convert while his Lebanese friends laugh at me. Along the same lines, according to Genoese Giacomo, who also converted: "The Catholic Church, the West and Christians have failed and cannot stand up to the true creed, which will advance and make it pay to all those who hindered it".

Those who convert to Christianity are to be stigmatised even more, according to others. "If my son abandons Islam and for the crusaders, I kick him out", threatens a Yemeni father, south-east of Rome. Referring to his brother, Rashid reveals that: "Since Rihda became a Christian, we no longer talk to him", because, as Salah points out in Milan, "if you leave Allah for a simple prophet [Jesus], you are not worthy to sit at the table with other Muslims".

Troubled, I investigate the matter in question with a member of a Lombard mosque:

"What happens if a person coming from the Islamic faith converts to Christianity?" I ask.

"It can't happen. If a person abandons Islam, that means he was never really Muslim".

"Okay, but what if it happens?".

"It is not acceptable anyway".

"But can a Christian person become a Muslim?".

"Sure, it's a fair and free choice".

"I don't want to be rude, but, similarly, if you have a Muslim who freely chooses to convert to another religion… isn't that the same thing?".

"No, it's very different".

"Why?"

"Because... it's totally different. Islam is perfect, it's for everyone. If you leave, it's a terrible offense against God".

Not only does this conversation show a certain doctrinal closemindedness and aversion to Christianity, but it also shows double standard. A Christian who converts to Islam is more than welcome, but despite living in Italy, the reverse is not acceptable at all.

Nevertheless, an experience in particular leaves me truly puzzled.

I walk out of this major Roman mosque after attending the sermon. It is late and I would love to go back to the hotel, but this very colourful stand run by one father and his son selling bracelets and necklaces catches my eye. As we start talking and laughing, a threatening looking man in his forties approaches me:

"Who are you?" He asks grumpily.

"Hi, I am Michele and I'm doing a research on Islam in Italy for my doctorate ..."

"On Islam?" He interrupts me.

"Yes, I would like to understand what Italian Muslims think about certain matters. Can I explain to you what the research is about?".

"But are you a Muslim?" the man cuts me off.

"I am a Christian".

"Bad".

"Do you want to participate in the study?", I ask after a brief hesitation.

"Yes, but only if you answer this question".

"Sure".

"If you believe that God created the world and that mankind is under God, and 'Muslim' actually means 'submitted to God', then we must all be Muslims. So, you are really a Muslim and you don't even realise that you continue to follow a false religion?", he says with superiority.

"Like all Christians, I believe what Jesus said".

"But I am more Christian than you are, and I know Jesus better than you; he is only a prophet who never said to be God".

"I am happy that you also consider yourself a good Christian, but, actually, the Bible is full of references and direct phrases that say the opposite, as in the Gospel of John", I replied.

"It is not true!".

"Yes, that's true, don't get angry".

"Apostate!", He shouts at me, pushing me.

You know, while unpleasant, it's not this minor physical aggression what troubles me most–also because the two people from stands intervene and stop the man. I'm not really shaken by the man's allegations of Christianity being "false" and me being "Apostate" either - I have atheist friends who question everything. Besides, though rude, these are the legitimate opinions of a man, who may be inclined to verbal quarrels, I would almost certainly share very little with.

Yet, I am fairly shocked by three things: the anger I see in this person's eyes, his inability to undertake a sincere theological conversation with me, and, above all, the arrogant lack of respect for the religion of the country where he lives and freely expresses (but in an ignorant way) his opinions. Although every confession counts arrogant individuals, I return to the hotel a bit discouraged–especially considering the fact that the previous week I was kicked out from another Milanese mosque without any explanation, even before I could speak to someone.

In addition to the Christian faith, some people's Muslim identity "quarrels" with various attitudes and customs of society, to the point they avoid non-Muslims. "My son cannot stay in Italian schools where gays and lesbians are celebrated, there are Christmas plays but not Ramadan; that's why I don't send him to school anymore ", explains a Somali father in Venice. "Now it is fashionable to accept homosexuals, Jews, atheists, divorced people, selfish women; better to be with those who pray to Allah and stay pure ", says Turkish Emre, near piazza Duomo, in Milan. In the same vein, an Egyptian man adds: "We Muslims still have values; here people lose themselves, become atheist, do what they want ... we stay only among ourselves, which is better!". "Not a chance... for my daughter, I just want a good Muslim boy, no Italians, no football shenanigans, beer and junk TV programmes", wishes one Cameroonian parent in Modena. As does Fatma in Bergamo, who feels horrified about the possibility that her daughter can wear "jeans and go to clubs with her friends".

Not only do some interviews show rejection of certain habits and customs, but they also feature the intention to "Islamise" and/or impose one's own belief in order to alter certain social dynamics. "Given that we are many, the school cafeteria should not serve pork, they should remove the cross from the classrooms, and only the male professors should do PTA meetings", claims a Senegalese father in Arcella, Padua. Indeed, as urged by Moosa, a Neapolitan Algerian student, "every school programme must have at least one hour of Islamic religion per week taught by Imams and should excuse students who leave classrooms to observe Ramadan".

"The locals must not sell alcohol at all and the police must stop drunk people, homosexuals and women with miniskirts showing their butt," continues Jawad in Reggio Emilia. Speaking of clothes, veils and "burkini", a converted woman invites all swimming pools in Bologna to "guarantee spaces and hours reserved for Muslim women who do not want to wear swimsuits or see other men". According to Noori, a Pakistani from Brescia, "all the mosques in Italy must have minarets for the call to the five daily prayers, otherwise, you only hear church bells". And, in the words of a Jordanian man in Via Padova, Milan: "In the beginning, there was a time to be Jewish, then a time to be Christian; now, for Italy, there is only time to be Muslim".

In order to safeguard Muslim customs and habits, others would impose Sharia, Islamic law. "5 Stars Movement, right, left ... as soon as we have the numbers, our goal is to form an Islamic party ... it seems obvious to me, right?", an Italian-Palestinian in Florence rhetorically asks. "Not only should crucifixes be removed from schools and squares, but Italy should approve polygamy, arranged marriages and other principles of [Islamic] law," urges Mansour, a Qatari cleric, in Brescia. According to Tariq in Turin, the introduction of Sharia "is only a matter of time, because in a few years we will be 50% of the population and we will change the law".

The conversation with a smiley Arab restaurateur near the Sforzesco Castle in Milan is also emblematic:

"Do you believe that things will improve for Muslims in Italy?" I ask.

"Absolutely yes, we will all be Muslims here one day! My wife, an Italian ex-Catholic, has converted to Islam. My children are Muslims and are Italian citizens. Muslims are having more and more children, more and more people are converting to Islam, you are becoming more and more atheist, and you don't have children. In some years, we will speak Arabic. Many women will cover their faces and bodies and you will work for us".

Irritating and chilling, such words show the (seemingly) latent desire by a segment of the Islamic community to change Italian society from within. This, however, would be done not through the establishment of shared commonalities, but by replacing every aspect of Italian culture with peculiar religious and social visions.

In addition to highly undemocratic attitudes, a further source of concern is embodied by conspiracy theories, which are spotted in 55% of the interviews (110/200).

Let us be clear. Having doubts is natural. Contesting predominant narratives and shady events is also legitimate. And, in itself, conspiracy theories do not automatically threaten social order or integration processes or societal feelings of belonging. But supporting theories based on factious logic that does not allow for any objective analysis, promoting hatred, crosses the line – especially if one considers the lack of respect for those who lost their lives due to criminal acts.

Having said this, conspiracy theorists' preferred topic is, of course, jihadist terrorism. As we will see in the following pages, most of the Italian Muslim community rejects violence in the name of God. "The terrorists are not true Muslims!" This is what is explained to me on almost every occasion.

Strong and resolute, this affirmation is not, however, always understood as a theological or ideological deviation by errant subjects. Having reached this stage of the interview, dozens of individuals conceive the phrase "the terrorists are not true Muslims "in its literal sense. That is, terrorists are not people from the Islamic faith, but mercenaries and elusive Jewish, American, British, etc. secret agents, disguised as Muslims in order to discredit Islam.

"Bin Laden and ISIS are controlled by the Mossad and Israel, who want to destroy the world," declare two Northern African waiters from Reggio Emilia. "It is obvious that ISIS cannot be made of Muslims," continues their friend Yasir, "because they are too physically fit; it is obvious that they are American football players, marines paid to tarnish the Muslims". Likewise, a Syrian citizen in Bologna believes that "Charlie Hebdo was an attack by American, Israeli and French secret services to bomb Syria more".

According to Pakistani Muhktar, there are even "English and Indians" behind ISIS attacks in Europe. For Afghani Umar, in Brescia, "Al Qaeda is an invention of the United States; it does not exist, just like Bin Laden and Daesh do not exist". In fact, in the words of the Neapolitan-Tunisian Yoonus, "few in the Arab world believe 9/11 and similar attacks happened because Muslims do not do things like that... others may because they are afraid of Islam and must find a way to make war on us and keep us under control". Perhaps it is not surprising, therefore, that in the polls almost 60% of the participants (259/440) think that 11/09 is an American-Jewish plot.

To a couple of people inside a Milanese bar, the bloody events of the Bataclan have never taken place. According to Andrea, a convert, and Mustafa, a Moroccan, there would not be any casualties. The Bataclan, like Charlie Hebed, would be a construction of the media, created ad-hoc for specific purposes.

Willing to overcome my visible scepticism, the two show me a video on YouTube. According to the film's authors, the blood splatter on the floor and on the walls would not coincide with the true dynamics of the shooting, while victims and perpetrators, would be nothing but simple actors:

"So, nothing happened that day?" I ask at the end of the video in an uncomfortable tone.

"No, everything was set up".

"What about that blood on the ground?".

"It's paint, as the ballistics expert in the video says".

"So, nobody died?".

"Not at all! They are all actors. It was like a movie".

"What about the actual footage of the shooting, witnesses, the people rushed to the hospital?".

"It's all fake! Televisions and newspapers are controlled by Jewish Free Masons and their bankers. They make you see things that are not true because they want to rule the world. It's all recorded and put together like on a movie set".

"Excuse me, but who did it then?".

"The Mossad and the Jewish bankers, I told you. There is a global plan against Islam. ISIS is a hoax founded by these people, who want to make Muslims look bad to invade the

Middle East, take the oil, keep all the Arabs divided, and let the Jews kill all the Palestinians".

Speaking of Jews, the role the latter play in tragic, criminal or controversial situations seems to be an obsession for dozens of conspiracy theorists. In the polls, 60% of the respondents (266/440) state that Jews control the world and are responsible for much evil. In the interviews, the Jewish people are indeed accused of controlling media and finance; of starting wars and diseases; of having devised a plan to counter the rise of Islam in the West.

From north to south, ranging from Senegalese to Indonesian citizens, remarks sound roughly the same:

"Jewish Free Masons control the banks and decide who is to be elevated and who is to be lowered"; "Jews are responsible for economic crises meant to control the world and kill Muslims in Iraq, Syria and Palestine"; "The Jews control all the newspapers and television stations in the world"; "Jews control schools, universities, CNN, the BBC and RAI"; "The Jews corrupt and buy the silence of the media and politicians over Israel"; "The Jews are behind the French revolution, the American one and the communist one "; "The Jews are behind what you call Arab Springs"; "The Jews brought the plague, AIDS and cancer to sell drugs and medicines"; "Jews are responsible for the Ebola virus"; "The Jews know that Islam will conquer the world and are waging war by inventing ISIS and Al Qaeda"; "The Jews plan a world plan against us to control the oil market and prevent the Arab world and Palestinians from becoming rich".

The theory of a Yemeni citizen in Catania perfectly sums up all the elements listed, adding, however, a rather particular one:

"By now everyone knows that Jews control the world, banks, schools, newspapers and television stations - and that they are behind every war and disease for economic interests. What not many know, however, is that Jews have also created Christianity. They already knew the Islam would come. So, what did they do? They took a man named Jesus, pretended to crucify him, and created Christians to sell Bibles and force them to fight against Muslims, to prevent the world from seeing the truth".

Though absurd, such conspiracy theories often give way to the most brazen anti-Semitic sentiment. Once again, from Como to Palermo, comments do not vary much: "Jews are cancer"; "Worse than Jews? Only dogs and mice"; "Jews are greedy and always try to deceive you and stab you in the back"; "Jews only think about money and have no qualms at all"; "If there is someone who creates problems and always complains, those are certainly Jews who always try not to pay"; "The Jews are so attached to money and to their lies that the wrath of God is upon them"; "The Jews are all destined to hell where Allah will punish them"; "Look at them, they have always brought wars and slander, how can you not hate them?".

Given our recent past, these expressions are worrying because we, more than others, know very well what they can bring about.

In conclusion, if by "integration" we mean the search for commonalities between Muslim identity and society, the community appears divided once again. On the one hand, we meet the various Kamals, who are Muslims full of happiness, gratitude, love and "desire" for Italy. On the other hand, we run into homophobic, sexist, absolutist, conspiracist, anti-Western and anti-Semitic feelings, lacking any compatibility with those values that the new generations try, with difficulty, to internalise.

So, what is the deal? Are Muslims in Italy integrated or are they not?

In my humble opinion, perhaps in simplistic terms, I think the answer is: "So and so".

Focus on Women, Second Generations, and Converts

Although they do not always enjoy constant media attention, women, second generations, and converts play an important role within the Italian Islamic community. Therefore, the following pages focus on the condition of each of these groups, highlighting dynamics and problems. For example, what does it mean to be a Muslim woman in Italy? How do second generations of Islamic citizens relate to Italian society? And how do Italian converts live?

Women

The condition of Muslim women is, in general, a quite sensitive subject. In a social context where moral (and sexual) conduct is a matter of irrevocable liberty, women's traditional Islamic outfit may cause discomfort. First of all, it visibly differs from feminine "Western" standards. Second, veil, burka and "burkini" can, at times, spark doubts and preconceptions about basic freedoms and the overall condition of Muslim women. Third, being automatically associated to Islam, traditional outfit can amplify society's perception of the Muslim presence in the country. For these reasons, the status of Muslim women is often matter of controversy.

In light of this, what do Muslim women think of their condition in Italy? What does it mean to be a Muslim woman today?

I can assure you that answering these questions is not always easy, though. If you cannot count on any personal contacts, approaching Muslim women in the street may prove to be complicated. Amongst those who I approach, many do not speak Italian. Feeling already in the spotlight because of their external appearance, it seems that a few want to avoid strangers like myself. In one particular case, I even get the feeling that this girl I am trying to establish a conversation with is actually fearful to be seen talking to me. And, finally, there are just far fewer Muslim women than Muslim men.

In line with demographic data at the national level, it is not surprising that, within the study, women are greatly outnumbered compared to men. In the surveys, female individuals amount to 30% of the sample (133/440), while in interviews to 25% (48/200).

However, once they overcome initial shyness and suspicion, it is in the interviews that women allow their big souls to emerge. Strong souls, which, maybe accustomed to suffering, share their experience with even more intimacy than their male counterparts. As such, I end up witnessing stories of faithfulness and courage, but I also end up reporting the kind of unease tied to the desire to defend and express one's identity, whichever that may be.

With this, however, I do not intend to generalise. There are Muslim women who, whether they are observant or not, live peaceful and pleasant lives. Aisha, for example, states that her Italian experience is devoid of any "problems and bad things". Likewise, Ana and her Indonesian friend say they do not really "care about everything that happens around ", for they live for "the family, without anyone disturbing us".

On the other hand, around 20 girls (40% of the interviewees) cannot help but share that very sense of malaise expressly linked to their external appearance. Respecting tradition, their outfit so often turns into source of unease within Italian society.

And the experience of Sarah, her mother and sister are a perfect example of the kind of tension that could arise.

I must be honest, but when we sit down inside this travel agency in Milan, I am the one who starts looking down. I have the privilege of traveling frequently. I've lived and I return to the Middle East. In England, where I work, there are many women who look like her. And yet, quiet and gentle, Sarah's mother makes me feel a bit awkward, for I rarely interact with women whose eyes are the only part of the body not to be covered.

Luckily, Sarah, a top student who wears the veil only, disregards my initial clumsiness vis-à-vis her mother's integral burka and spits it all out:

"We no longer even notice it, but everyone, wherever we go, stares at us," tells Sarah. "And let's not even mention my mother. I see the people in the street; everyone looks at her as if she were an alien, a mummy, or even a dog. And this happens when we all go out together as well. We go to the movies? Everybody is staring. We hop on the tube? Everyone is staring. We go shopping? I've even seen a few employees look at us with suspicion, as if they were asking themselves 'What are they hiding? Are they carrying a bomb under their clothes? Will they steal anything?'. Is it so hard to understand that we want to be and look like this? For us, our veil, and for my mother her integral burka, is a pleasure, a choice that we make because we believe in God and respect our fathers and husbands. We are not beaten, and we are not mistreated. We are not stupid or backward. It is a sign of our commitment; it is a question of identity. This is us. But then, we hear talking about freedom and that we are not free; regardless, can I be free to choose how to dress myself, even if I don't dress like the others? I don't hurt anyone, and like my mother and sister, I too have my right to be a Muslim and walk in the street without constantly feeling at the zoo".

Passionate and tenacious, Sarah's words reinforce testimonies from other interviewees, challenging preconceptions of coercion and subjugation of women in Islam.

Like Sarah, Nawal, Rachida and Mariam also maintain that their external look is not a constriction by someone else; rather, it is a free and conscious choice, in full compliance with the democratic values of society. "I have a brain, I study, and I am able to take care of myself. Even if others do not dress like me, I choose to be like this, for my clothes speak of what I believe", tells Fatma. "My mother does not want me to wear the veil, but I like it and I want to decide for myself, as everyone does," says Rachida. To Miriam, her veil is a "democratic right; there are people who dress like jocks, others like punks, others like rappers ... I like wearing a veil and a long skirt, what's the problem? A question of security? Oh please!".

According to other girls, their aesthetic aspect is not only a choice, but a personal duty towards God. For example, another woman named Aisha preaches how "every good Muslim daughter, girl and wife must dress with dignity for Allah". Likewise, an elderly lady in Reggio Emilia educates me as to how Muslim women should not tempt men: "Allah teaches us that the eye is evil and leads to sin; therefore, we must show respect and grace so as not to let men sin; this is our noble mission". "God tells us to cover ourselves and a woman, provided she has true faith, must obey ", concludes Yana.

A more conservative outfit is also perceived as a means for personal safety. Especially at night, "there are so many drunk and funny looking men… having the veil protects me more," explains Takwa. Maybe ashamed of her physical appearance, Cala instead describes her experience at the pool as "traumatic", and that is why her "burkini" grants her "more confidence and safety". Along the same lines, Maleka reveals that when they "go to the sea, I am always afraid because I feel people always stare at me; that's why I prefer long and black swimsuits and I don't care if the other women look at me badly".

Finally, other Muslim women debunk stereotypes of violence, backwardness, and submission commonly associated to traditional outfit. "If you see a girl in the street wearing a veil, that does not mean that she has a husband who beats her; see, I have a veil, I am single, and no one mistreats me" jokes Yasmine. For Jalilah, who is married with children, the veil is" a contract, a symbol of loyalty, respect and love, not a gesture of arrogance and strength: my husband takes care of me and we make decisions together, as I believe many Italian women do. "Irritated but eloquent is Lulu's comment: "Where do we live? I was practically born in Italy and they taught me that you can't judge a book by its cover; so why does this not apply to us Arab women? At home, I get nothing but love and attention. My husband is a fantastic man. We love and respect each other with or without veil. He has never laid a finger on me, in fact, I was the one who once beat him up".

For Abal, more traditional outfits would even be the last frontier of feminism:

"Italian and Western society is hypocritical. Many women say they are feminists, but that is not true. Italian women are still objects available to men. So, imagine if men are robbed of their desire to objectify women; no more heals and mini-skirts, just the face. Unrestrained sex and divorces would naturally decrease as people would look into their hearts and get married for love".

While they still take pride and identity in their veils and burkas, other women see traditional clothes as reason for anxiety. To start with, traditional outfit might entice public subtle attitudes that undermine one's confidence. "As I always take the bus and the subway, do you know how many times I feel looked upon with suspicion or superiority just because I wear the veil? "asks Hafa. "I don't understand, I see ugly people on the train, including drug addicts; yet, I must be worse than them because I always get other peoples' eyes on me", reiterates Takwa.

In other cases, physical appearance might also trigger tangible acts of discrimination, especially at the workplace. In practical terms, the choice to wear veil and other traditional clothes could hinder hiring, recruiting, and better salaries. To such regard, Rafa's and Yusra's job interviews are meaningful examples of this:

"Michele, I had to refuse three jobs because they asked me, before hiring me, if I could get rid of my veil. What was I then doing at university? Why did I finish and graduate if what truly matters is not how good I am, but what I wear and how I pray? I finally gave up and decided to do something different, for I got fed up getting hurt", recalls Rafa.

"A former employer of mine said this to me: 'I am not a racist, but our customers would not feel at ease with the veil you wear and, thus, if there are no problems for you, we would like you to dress in a more proper way. If you don't want to change your appearance, we can offer you a desk job in the office, but for less money'. In that moment, I felt like he spat on my identity, stealing my soul', sadly reminisces Yusra.

Women's unease is not only due to the difficulty to strike a good balance between societal aesthetic expectations and one's religious identity. A dozen interviewees (25% total out of 200 cases) illustrate how this type of malaise might also come from within one's own Islamic community. On one side, sexist and misogynist attitudes may compromise healthy relationship between men and women. On the other side, more traditionalist visions clash with the idea that women may abandon or reshape certain Islamic customs and habits, for the latter might be considered outdated or unfit vis-à-vis the current zeitgeist.

Whilst based on Islamic concepts of loyalty and respect, certain women's relationship with their husbands could turn out to be fairly turbulent. Certainly, this might also be true for most couples. Probably, for whatever reason, all couples, at a certain point, have minor or major issues. Regardless of religion and social/historical context, it is a solid fact that large segments of the population experience marital problems. Hence, I categorically reject any automatic assumption and linkage between Islam and women's suffering. Nevertheless, I believe there are acts of sexism, humiliation, and abuse that must not be ignored.

Since I do not believe in fate, I don't think it is a coincidence that, while wandering around the peninsula, I end up witnessing one of these stories.

It's a mild afternoon in Naples. As I stroll around the picturesque narrow and noisy alleys, I breathe in the scent of the sea. The day following the trip to the Senegalese market (the one I shared two chapters ago), I am ever so content. It's finally good to see how whomever comes to Italy with nothing can make it despite objective harshness. Celebrating by eating a "panuozzo", I get really thirsty and I realise the time has come for a nice cold drink. I spot and then enter a small grocery store. I notice that a Pakistani family, made of a father, a mother and a daughter in her twenties, runs the shop –no worries, I am only assuming they are a family because the girl looks exactly like her father.

I ask for a Coca-Cola. Not being very tall, the lady climbs up the huge fridge behind the counter. But once he reaches the drink, she drops it, making much noise. Her husband, who is carefully supervising the operation, instead of helping her, starts yelling at her. Regrettably, I do not speak Pashto or Urdu, but it does not take a genius to understand that those are insults. For ten long seconds, the woman takes it all without blinking. Embarrassed, I quietly intrude saying that there is really no problem:

"Please don't worry, I'll drink the Coke anyway, it's okay", I reassure the father.

"Sorry, I'll get you another Coke," replies the father.

"No problem, really ..."

"You know, woman ... stupid, stupid woman ... not able to do anything, for she's useless; I hope your wife is better than this one here".

Now. I would lie to you if I told you I've never treated my mother or my wife poorly. Unfortunately, that happens to me too. And when I calm down, I usually feel shame, end up regretting it, and apologise. Hence, I cannot know if the man was having a bad day, nor can I know if he later apologised. But I understand from the daughter's look upon her face, staring down, that something is wrong. Feeling guilty, I come up with an excuse and I ask her to show me the way to the train station; once outside, I can't help but apologise for what my Coca-Cola had just caused:

"Look, forgive me, I could have asked for the water that was there at hand," I say with sorrow.

"Don't worry", the girl replies kindly.

"No, I'm sorry".

"Well, it happens all the time ... he treats her bad".

"Eh, look, it happened to me too".

"Yes, but my father always does this with mom, and not just him. In our culture, women must keep quiet, for men are always right, even if they are bad. That's not fair".

Similar feelings are also shared on the other side of the country. Speaking cautiously of the condition of women within the Islamic community, Fatma and Ara, from Como, echo their Neapolitan pier: "If you don't agree with men, it's over; all my friends, who are good, faithful, Allah-serving women, are unhappy because men are just selfish", says Fatma. "I am lucky enough, but my sisters can never say anything; they cook and do the ironing, for their husbands never lift a finger, never help with the cleaning, never ask how others are doing, never buy anything for the house…and still, if something at home is out of place, they insult their wives and their children, even if I am standing there too", reports Ara.

In truth, according to two interviewees, certain men would even use certain women's benign and faithful nature to justify sexist behaviours. Near Piazza della Signoria in Florence, Dalal reveals that: "In Islam, women must respect their husbands and, so, many women do so; men, however, take advantage of this and tell us women that we must shut up and do what they want". These situations might cause resentment and sense of inferiority towards men, as Asra articulates in Bergamo:

"We are their slaves! This is why I divorced my husband here in Italy… that bastard! He says he is a Muslim, but he is not. Islam means respect and love. But, for him, I was nothing; he was nice at the beginning, he seemed he would treat me better than the Queen of England and then, instead, it was a nightmare. He didn't care about me, he made me feel a dirty toilet, where he could spit and shit whenever he wanted. And so many males are like that. Everyone knew, but no one in the mosque has ever said anything to him. Because we are not allowed to say anything and, since we are good and we wear the veil, men take advantage of all of us. But one day, all this will change!".

Other instances show how freedom of choice and respect might be conditional to the adherence to specific habits and customs. For two female students in Rome and Milan, rejection of arranged marriages, for example, is source of great unease and bitterness. The story of Randa, a Roman university student, is particularly sad: "I left home because I didn't want to go back to Bangladesh to marry a stranger my family elected for me; at that point, feeling dishonoured, my father had threatened to drag me on to the plane, so I left".

Similarly, Sanaa criticises polygamous attitudes by some family members: "We live in Milan and Italian law prohibits having multiple wives; we are not in Saudi Arabia and I would never want to live like this … I am not an object that can be used and exchanged when you get bored. When I tried to tell this to a number of relatives, they insulted me so badly … to the point that my father and my mother can no longer go to family dinners and lunches, just for my remarks".

More generally, desire for greater emancipation, whether that might be cultural and / or professional, is not always welcome within the Muslim community. I have the opportunity to talk about this with a Venetian-Italian Tunisian girl on a train to Rome:

"I love my family; But do you know how much I have to quarrel and cry to study, go out, have a drink and return home back a bit later at night? I do not want to become like my mother. I am grateful to my parents for allowing me to study, but that is the precisely the point: does it make any sense if, right now, I am not able to do things that my parents, including my father, did not have the chance to do? Wouldn't that be a contradiction? But we are closed-minded and if a woman tries to be different, to do something different, like studying, not wearing her veil, but wearing short skirts, everyone turns against her. And do you know why? Because men are afraid of us women becoming more independent to the point, they can no longer treat us as inferior beings".

Alarmingly, close-minded rejection to aspirations of greater freedom of choice and emancipation might even turn into physical abuse.

Before we go on, I would like to say that, given its sensitivity and actuality, my research refrains from addressing domestic violence. Besides, the latter also affects large amounts of Italian, non-Muslim women. As such, I believe us non-Muslim Italian males would be not credible if we started pointing fingers at our male Muslim counterparts.

But in a totally involuntary way, I do come across a first-hand case of domestic abuse. Probably in her forties, I spot a woman outside a major mosque in Rome. She's sitting with her arms folded and wears no veil. I am attracted by her posture: simple, but elegant. This woman seems strong, I can tell from her fierce eyes. As I approach her, I notice several passers-by looking at her funny; but she doesn't seem to care and, all at the sudden, tells me what she really thinks:

"I feel sorry for all these people. I feel sorry for them because they've never questioned anything about religion. And think that my mother, who's in there too, feels sorry for me. Now we can only see each other here, because I can't go back home anymore, for they decided not to speak to me anymore. This is because I wanted to go to college and stop wearing the veil and believe in God. Nobody says this. But in our culture, even more so if you are a woman, you can't be an atheist… they broke my nose, they forbade me to go to the hospital, and they locked me in my room. I ran away and I'm never going back. There's something extremely wrong if a religion allows these things to happen and if the very same women who suffer all of this don't say anything".

Considering this story, I want to reiterate it once more. Dramatic and courageous, this testimony should not be considered, however, as every Muslim woman's condition in Italy. Thank goodness, not all women (Christian or Muslim) are victims of physical and psychological violence. Not all husbands, partners, and family members impose sexist visions. And not all Muslim women are forced to defend their Islamic identity on a daily basis. Essentially, not all Muslim women in Italy suffer and live unhappy lives. Indeed, I am quite convinced that, for many, the opposite is true.

On the other hand, the fact that most of the interviewees I interact with feels the need to share what causes discomfort is indicative. Because, perhaps, us males take feminine feelings for granted. Because, perhaps, us males often forget women have opinions and aspirations too. Because, whether within the Italian society or the Islamic community, us men seldom forget that women are here, with their own identity and voice.

And I think this is exactly the point. Despite the many difficulties, Muslim women fight and will continue to fight for their identity and the role that they want to cover, whichever that might be, wherever that might be. And no sexist man or social injustice is going to discourage them.

Second Generations

Let's face it. When we think of Islam in Italy, we often associate it with foreign people. We imagine them coming for faraway places made of mountainous and deserted landscapes. We picture them inside Kebab shops speaking Eastern languages, smoking hookahs.

Perhaps, we find it harder to imagine Alì serving ossobuco dishes speaking Lombard idiom like actor Renato Pozzetto. Perhaps, we do not imagine Shadiya selling red radicchio in Venetian dialect. And, perhaps, we do not imagine Mohammed doing a super realistic impression of TV character Gabibbo. Yet, these are just some of the young people I encounter during my journey: they are "second-generation" Muslim girls and boys who were born in Italy.

Even though they do not receive constant media attention, second generations are so often caught in the struggle between integration and security. Both the acquisition of citizenship and homegrown terrorism, for instance, inflame the debate around these young people. For many, bills such as Ius Soli would facilitate the inclusion of thousands of Muslims born in Italy, granting them citizenship and a much-sought sense of belonging. Aware of some neighbouring European nations' experience, a section of the public fears such inclusive measures may instead lead to loss of identity, social instability, and terrorism - especially because second generations are statistically the most likely to be affected by violent radicalisation leading to terrorism against one's own country.

Although we are not able to contribute to such debates, I cannot help but wonder: how do second generations of Muslim citizens relate to Italian society? And what does it mean to be a young Muslim, or a young Muslim born in Italy?

In truth, it would be fascinating to undertake a study exclusively aimed at hundreds of these young Muslims born here. On the other hand, while captivating, this hypothetical research would not faithfully represent the demographic composition of the Islamic community. Contrary to other continental realities (such as France), most of the Muslim population in Italy is mainly composed of first-generation foreigners. Ergo, in tune with data at the national level, the study's second-generation Muslims born in Italy, whether they hold citizenship or not, amount to 17% in the surveys (76/440) and to 20% in the interviews (37/200).

It is fair to specify, however, that these figures are also the result of the relativity of the term in question and of a personal choice. Dozens of participants were not born in Italy. Still, they have been living here since an early age. As a result, these young people go to school, have friends in the neighbourhood, play football, and work in our country. Hence, in practical terms, these young people are actually part of the "second generation" despite being born abroad. However, for a statistical matter, I prefer to include only those subjects who were physically born in Italy.

That said, similarly to the above mentioned women, the interviews offer valuable insights as of the lives of second-generation Muslims. These are courageous young people.

Young people who speak as adults. Who face the kinds of challenges and problems already elucidated. Who look at the future determined to carve out their own space in society? Who feel Italians and speak with regional accents and dialects? Who wish to contribute to the growth of the country?

Feeling proud Italians, it is not surprising that the vast majority of respondents (31/37) actively works to build bridges between the Islamic community and Italian society.

In relation to Italy, these young people feel the duty to clarify and contextualise Islamic principles, which are often unknown, misunderstood, and deemed as lack of freedom, close-mindedness, and fanaticism. "We were born here, and we are Italians", says Nadia in Milan. "We cannot let society and Muslims misunderstand each other, because we have a duty to help everyone understand everyone in order to live better".

In doing so, however, none of the interviewees criticises and judges Italian society. Intended to make people understand the complexity of Islam as a religion, young people like Abdullah from Turin preach openness and proactive approaches:

> "Islam is a complex religion, like Christianity. This is what I always try to explain to my friends; today, there are many people, Muslims and non-Muslims, who always try to see things black and white, but reality is never like that. We must be open. My task, at the workplace as much as at the bar, is to make people think and see the complexity of several matters. It is very important that society realises this, because only by appreciating diversity can people understand and respect each other more and more. But if we want to

help society understand us, given that we are the ones who were born here, we are the ones who have to take the initiative".

Putting this exhortation into practice, several young people apply their energies to educate the public as for widespread preconceptions about daily prayer and festivities, physical appearance, eating habits, and violence in the name of God.

"I can understand why people get frightened if they see Muslims praying in the street, dressed differently, saying prayers in Arabic ... we're not in Casablanca," says Basel, born in Bergamo, in a comprehensive way. "But if you see someone who prays, that doesn't mean that they are fundamentalist or madmen who are about to blow themselves up. I too pray, but I was born here; how could I hurt someone from my own city? Through public prayer, a person commits to showing his faith in Allah, seeking a personal relationship with Him. Therefore, it is not an attempt to impose something or, worse, to plot an attack. It is only a personal need to talk to God".

Likewise, Bolognese Fareed compares the meaning of the Islamic prayers to the Catholic ones: "For us 'Allah Akbar', that is, 'God is great', does not mean that we are about to perpetrate a crime or a murder, but that expression is similar to my Christian friends' Holy Father". "I know it is not easy to understand Ramadan, here in today's Italy," admits Venetian Azhar. "It may seem like something mandatory with a backward vibe, but we take Ramadan as an opportunity for personal and spiritual growth, something to do with friends and, above all, with the family". According to Khalid, from Catania, Islamic holidays in general represent a great opportunity for dialogue and brotherhood: "People worry when they see us observe Ramadan and sing all together; but there is no need to be afraid, we always invite everyone to eat with us, just as Italians give us pastries at Christmas, New

Year's Eve and Ferragosto. It's the same thing for us, that is, an opportunity to love each other and stay together".

As for women, male traditional outfits and different food habits would not necessarily be product of close-mindedness. On the contrary, they embody matters of respect and affection, contends Irfaan, a big young man wearing a long white dress, near Prato della Valle, Padua. His observations are similar to those of the women interviewed previously:

> "Sometimes I do feel people are starting at me, for sure. Yes, there are many women wearing veils and many brothers wearing long dresses, but nobody should be alarmed, because, once again, can't judge a book by its cover ... the dress per se is not the important thing. What is important is what the dress actually stands for, that is, a sign of respect not only for God, but also for others, a sign of love for my wife, a sign of respect for my father, a sign of respect for my city, which is Padua. I know that people do not dress like me, but my appearance helps me, because it reminds me of my daily struggle against sin and my commitment to becoming a better person every day. It is not a sign of backwardness; on the contrary, it forces me to look ahead. And when those who know me, finally understand we can all go beyond outfits and respect each other for who we are rather than how we dress, then I've done my job".

Along the same lines, Makeen, from Modena, reassures that the decision to avoid ham and sausages does not imply dogmatic restriction, but democratic freedom of choice:

> "You know, nobody forces me to avoid pork. My father doesn't beat me if I devour one peperoni pizza. And I don't judge others or look down on people because they eat pork. Nobody goes to Hell because they eat sausages, God goes beyond these things. I don't feel superior, but

I do feel it is my choice to eat what I prefer best, as, you know, I can choose, and Muslims can make decisions too. Even if I was born in the most famous area there is in this regard, I've never had any problems! I have always taken part to school dinners; sure, my schoolmates have asked me about my eating habits, but no one has ever treated me poorly for that ... because they have understood that I am not here to change their habits, and I can still participate and have fun with others. Besides, what's going to happen if I eat a salami sandwich? Are they going to strip me of my citizenship?".

In addition to this, the young people I meet are unanimous in condemning violence in the name of Islam. "People are afraid, and so are we, because, if terrorists blow themselves up in the tube, we die too. But let me just say that these are not true Muslims, for Islam means peace. These people are just criminals who know nothing about Islam and God in general. How can you think of going to Heaven by killing innocents?", asks Ashraf in his grocery store in Rome. Amjad, a Milanese Italian-Jordanian man, is also resolute: "Maybe you didn't understand; If I catch people from ISIS, I call the police and ask them to throw the keys away, for they pollute Islam not knowing anything about it, because no religion, anywhere in the world, tells you to kill people".

Several interviewees apply their energies for the creation of professional bridges and partnerships. Their ambition is not only fuelled by greater economic expectations; it also stems from the immense sense of gratitude these people have towards Italy. For instance, Faris, from Reggio, is so happy to work for a company that "helps all those struggling at finding occupation". Dawoud, from Palermo, is also proud of "having studied in one of the best Italian universities" and is looking forward to "opening a large business to serve everyone who needs financial consulting and assistance". Aisha, a charity worker, is glad to offer two Roman elderly citizens "a taste of Moroccan happiness and cuisine". And Wid, an Arabic native speaker working for an import-export company, feels enthusiastic to "increase sales and trade agreements between Italy and the Middle East".

Noteworthy is also Hassan's community work in Milan:

"What do you do in life, Hassan?".

"I assist homeless, refugees, and immigrants with our volunteering neighbourhood group".

"Congratulations! Who is part of this group?".

"Well, people who have been friends since childhood, plus other friends from Southern Italy who moved to Milan a while ago".

"You mentioned that you help immigrants too, correct?".

"Yes, that's right".

"If I may ask, which migrant groups touch you the most? If there are any."

"Syrians and Eritreans. You can see everything they've gone through in their eyes".

"Forgive my question, but, being a fellow Muslim, do you feel a special duty to help them?".

"If you talk about how my faith can entice action, then, yes; but if you are inferring that I only help them or feel more sympathetic just because they are Muslims, then, no. I help anyone I can. I was born here, at school I was taught that, no matter who you are, what the colour of your skin is, and what you believe in, we are one…we all often forget about that, but

I hope that even small bits of charity can show that each one of us can do his/her part to improve things".

Finally, other interviewees are not really clear as of what their role in society is, but they still can dream of becoming cultural icons. Hussein, another youngster from Milan, is visibly in love with rap and, as such, would love becoming a star like rapper Ghali: "Man, what I would do to be like him! He is Italian, he is Tunisian, but he loves everyone and everyone loves him back… he writes his music, he makes you think, he is entertaining … he is the living proof that even people like us can make it to the top!".

Being a footballer in Florence, Isaam dreams of becoming the next Stephan El Shaarawy: "El-Sha's story is just so cool! It shows that one man, who was born here and was raised by foreign Muslim parents, can indeed make it to Serie A and play for the national team, hopefully leading the nation to triumph. If I ever make it too, that would be my greatest thank you to Italy!".

Meant to facilitate integration, other young Italian Muslims focus their efforts on "modernising" certain professional traits within the Islamic community. Founders of a small cultural association in Bologna, Muayid and Omran offer free Italian and IT courses. Their aim is to increase and improve the skills of dozens of Arab families who live in Italy: "You can't live in Italy and not even know the language. That is not good for our integration, nor is it good for occupation, so, we decided it was time to give something back to both our communities," explains Omran. "Today everything is digital, but many people do not even know how to use a PC and they struggle at filling in tax returns, pay for bills and fines, make online reservations, download certain software, or register for a university online programme: that's what we are here for, to bridge this technological gap, helping everyone integrate better", recapitulates Muayid.

The word "brave" can describe what three other young Italian Muslims are up to. Sayid, Taref, and Subhy, all in their twenties, dedicate their time to ensure certain religious principles that openly clash with today's Italy are abandoned or re-contextualised. "Perhaps I am too sensitive about this, but we live in a free society and we have the responsibility to combat a the type of obscurantism we see towards women, gays, and other religions ... this intolerance and hatred are inhumane and do not belong to Italy or the kind of Islam many of us believe in", says Sayid.

It is no coincidence that, according to Tareef: "The struggle is for the creation of an Islam that can work here, today, in Italy. Let me be clear, I'm not saying that the Koran is false and that we must not follow the Prophet, but we are Italians and we cannot live like thousands of years ago in the Arabian desert. Ways and means must go hand in hand with the democratic environment that surrounds us, as we still maintain our faith". Maybe less diplomatic, Yarah, a Roman student, urges Muslims to "abandon the Middle Ages and pave the way for an Islamic Renaissance and Enlightenment, devoid of obscenities and various bullshit ... if we do not open our eyes, we will never advance, we will always remain ignorant, hated and mocked by all, at the mercy of dictators, petrol, and crooked politics".

In this respect, a young man who grew up in northern Italy expresses his joy as he recalls the time when he signalled a radicalised individual to the proper authorities:

"I saw this guy brainwashing people in the mosque into going to Syria and fight the infidels. I reported him to the police. It was my duty, as a Muslim and as an Italian… I had the chance to cleanse the community. Because we don't want these people, they disgust us, they don't represent us, they have to go back to their home. Here, we are lucky to live in a free country, not like in our parents' countries. So, if you have to come here to destroy and preach hatred, just go home, we are the first ones who do not want these things".

While many young people strive to create cultural bridges and look at the future with hope, there are others who, whilst born in Italy, do not have the same positive feelings. Amir is one of these. Scruffy looking, it seems he doesn't care about much. His eyes are disillusioned and turned off. Born in the south but raised in Veneto by Tunisian parents, Amir does not feel any sense of belonging, for he is in search of his own identity, which is sadly trapped between two worlds:

"When I look at what's out there –less and less values, people fighting and suing each other, junk TV, escorts, smoking, drugs, alcohol and clubbing… all this makes me sick. What kind of society can call itself as such when it allows all this, where those who have money exploit the weak and where people who flee wars on boats and die at sea get discriminated against? But then I come home and look at my parents and uncles. They came here as labourers, they've gained always the same check, repeating the same thing over and over, just to be looked down upon other people who were like them 50. And all of this, for what? To eat cheap couscous, pray five times a day, and marry a distant cousin because that pleases my aunt? Well, it seems to me it's all the same tape, over and over, and I don't really know what to watch on TV anymore".

Obviously, not all those trapped between cultures fall prey to identity issues. Many people who disagree with society and religious belief scan build unique and alternative identities. However, for individuals like Amir, it is clear that different worlds might cause pain and stillness.

Sometimes it gets even worse, as it is for Ubay, who, contrary to Amir, is stigmatised by both society and the Islamic community: "Even though I was born here, I have always been different. When I was a child, no one wanted to play football with me. Today, people still don't sit next to me on the bus or on the bench at the park, and even some "friends" talk behind my back because I am not married yet. Even if I attend mosque, my Imam has often humiliated me in front of everyone because I don't know the verses of the Koran by heart; I always do Ramadan, but other "brothers" still look at me funny because once I didn't feel good, I was about to faint and, so, I ended up eating a small candy. Since then, I've been mistreated and treated as a second-class Muslim. So, as you can see, on one side I am not Italian enough, and on the other side, I am not Muslim enough. Please just tell me which kind of person you'd all like me to be".

Unlike those searching for themselves, I encounter other young individuals who do boast a strong identity, but who are at war with society. These subjects' purpose is not the creation of an Italian Islam. They are not looking for common ground or shared experiences. They do not wish to build bridges between worlds. What these people want is, instead, changing Italian culture and Islamise the country.

To my surprise, Nooh and Idris tell me that right in my face: "It's not a coincidence that we were born here. We speak Italian to manifest Allah and facilitate people's return to Islam. And it's only a matter of time, no violence is needed, now that game's over. By now, there are already so many mosques and halal places where Italians convert... one day the whole country will pray to Allah ", foresees Nooh. "All schools must teach Islam and abandon the Christian religion, especially because in a few years Italian Muslims will be more than Italian non-Muslim. Sooner or later, everything, really everything, will change in this country - language, eating, clothing ... ", Idris reiterates.

Particularly disturbing (and irritating) is the conversation I have with Ismael, who, after explaining to me various Islamic principles, openly shares his ambitions:

"So, where do you see yourself in the coming years?" I ask him.

"Allah put me here to change people".

"What do you mean?".

"Everyone, including you, must submit to Allah".

"Submit?".

"Yes, to Allah"

"Don't you think people have the right to believe what they want?".

"What you say brings you to Hell".

"Maybe... but keep in mind that many people are Christian, others are atheists or agnostics ..."

"Not for long".

"That is?".

"Come on, the Catholic Church knows very well that Italy and the Vatican do not have many years ahead of them. The truth is emerging and, even if good Popes and crosses are put up there, people will see the true light. Nobody can stop us ...".

"But, excuse me, you were born here ...", I interrupt him a bit annoyed.

"I must say what I think, sorry, don't take it personally, but I was born here to change everything that is wrong".

"And what's wrong exactly?".

"Many, many things, from beer to clubbing, from Christmas to women who act as sluts".

"I too disagree with many things, but we live in a democracy".

"Which is made up of corrupt politicians who only follow the money and think of going to Heaven ... we all must convert to Allah, even the government".

"But theocratic governments have been problematic too, even ours in the past".

"But that's because Italy didn't follow the true God. When it will, everyone will be blessed ... at school, at work, everywhere".

"Not sure if that's going to happen.".

"Who knows, we'll talk about it in a few years when we are the majority and we are going to make the laws".

Fortunately, such controversial words are not generally supported. Most of the people I interact with were either born here or have being living here for years. These individuals feel Italian, are thankful, and want to contribute and give "something back". Ergo, these are the people we should be looking for. It's on these guys both society and the community should invest in, for they sincerely strive for dialogue. If they are not assisted, however, they might end up being overshadowed by other peers who have nothing or little to do with Italy and its culture.

Whatever happens, second-generation Italian Muslims are surely destined to play a crucial role in tomorrow's Italy.

Converts

We do not exactly know how many Italian converts our country features. Unofficial estimates range from 50 to 100 thousand individuals, forming from 2% to 4% of the overall Islamic population. My study counts 40 40 in surveys (out of 440, which is 9% of the total) and 8 in interviews (out of 200, which is 4%).

Regardless of the number, conversion to Islam incarnates a delicate issue. This is because, perhaps most of all, Italian converts concretely embody fears of identity loss and attempts of Islamisation by definition. Further, whilst converts form small segments of many Western Islamic communities, they are overrepresented in jihadist attacks. Comparably less than other European realities, Italy too reports bellicose converts who left for Syria and Iraq. Among these, Giulia Delnevo and Maria Giulia Sergio (alias Fatima) are still alive in the Italian memory, especially for the type of resentment towards her country of origin.

Given the type of potential uncertainty surrounding them, what do the examined converts think about their condition? What does it mean to be a convert in Italy?

Though we should keep in mind that the study features only a few converts, we can still get very different answers to the above questions. For four respondents, conversion is not just about inner peace and happiness. It is also what motivates one's proactive behaviours and attitudes aimed at both mainstream society and the Islamic community itself.

Whilst not particularly fond of Italian media, Alessandro, from Marche, cannot help but sharing his gratitude: "Before

I converted, I was unhappy; now, I am the happiest person in the world, and I owe it both to those who brought me the Koran, and to my country that allows me to live in peace and harmony with all". Mario, a former Roman soldier, is also filled with joy when he relives his spiritual journey: "I saw what war looks like, I saw countless bad things, but then Allah gave me back my life, gave me confidence again, and I now see Rome, my family, and everything more beautiful and amazing than ever!".

Similarly, to the young people born in Italy from last section, other two converts apply their energies to build bridges between Italy and Islam. Giacomo, a merchant from Turin, really believes that he must help foreign families learn Italian: "I do my best to teach Italian to all foreigners, both as a tool of integration and as a tool of knowledge, so that nobody can manipulate and brainwash potentially vulnerable subjects".

Similarly, Francesco, from Calabria, claims converts must help the Islamic community find the so-sought entente with the Italian State: "Us converts are the glue between two worlds and it's up to us to work and bring together immigrants, foreigners, workers and Italians ... because, knowing the two realities well, I believe that it is our task to seek an official agreement with the State, showing the Italian people that there is nothing to fear, for we all have the same dreams and fears".

Chiara's situation is, instead, completely different. A Milanese convert, I mentioned Chiara two chapters ago. For this woman, conversion has been and continues to be source of suffering: "Since I've converted, my mother no longer speaks to me. I am still very attached to her, but now she won't even answer the phone and I cry every day; I am not changing my mind, but saying that, for me, it's easy to wear the veil, be myself, and be totally happy, is a big lie".

Andrea, whom I've also quoted previously, struggles too. A Sicilian convert living in Milan, his conversion is what caused his divorce:

"I was looking for God and I couldn't find him; when Allah finally allowed me to see Him, it was the best day of my life; but the next day, it was the worst day of my life, when my wife told me that she could not accept my new religion, saying that, if we wanted to stick together, I would have to abandon my God ... I have tried everything to make it all work, but, a few months later, she left me and now I have to fight to see my children, who are my life ... I have to stay strong, but, sometimes, I would like to ask everyone in Italy, including all of her friends, if they see themselves as tolerant people… because it seems to me, they are not".

Besides stories of happiness and pain, I also run into stories of anger and resentment. Diametrical to the kind of happiness shared by some above mentioned converts, Giacomo's underlying hatred towards Italy cannot go unnoticed: "I hate this hypocrisy by society, the West, America, Israel, may that country be damned, the Catholic Church, and all those who vote right…they all make me laugh; if you believe priests and some other people, you must be that stupid".

It is no coincidence that Luca, former leftist activist from Varese, brings to the question whether his conversion to Islam might be just another banner under which he can continue his antagonistic struggle: "I converted because Islam is, by definition, the religion of the oppressed, for no one can actually be submitted, unless you are submitting to Allah ... on the contrary, we will never be slaves! So, no government, no police, no fascists, no politicians, no Jews, no bankers, no man-made rules…there's only Allah ... capitalism and America, which are this world's cancers, will fall under the blows of Islam".

Though these are only a few cases, it is clear that the reasons for conversion are multiple and inherently intimate. On top of it, we are unable to know how many Italians are going to convert to Islam in the near future. But what we can see already is that dialogue with converts is crucial for social cohesion. In other words, if we forget about converts, not only would we lose an opportunity to approach Islam in Italy through the lenses of individuals who are, arguably, more in tune with mainstream society; we might also pave the way for people like Giacomo and Luca. Given the possible degrees of uncertainty awaiting us, I think missing this chance might be unwise.

Radicalisation and Terrorism

Killing in the name of God

It's true. If we look at the data, terrorism kills less people than that malaria, cardiovascular diseases, and road accidents caused by reckless use of mobile phones while driving.

It's true. Numerically, separatist attacks still outnumber jihadist attacks. According to Europol data, every year in Europe, ETA and similar groups still perpetrate more attacks than ISIS.

And it's true. Radicalism does not automatically equate to terrorism. Those who advocate "radical" or orthodox Islamic ideas (I say "Islamic", but from any creed, really), for the most part, never turn violent. While several jihadist terrorists are not even observant.

Let's not pretend it's all good, however. While it is necessary to contextualise them, we shouldn't be afraid to state that jihadist radicalisation and terrorism do frighten us. The jihadist cause radicalises and attracts thousands of men and women. In the name of God, jihadist attacks aim to be, generally, the most lethal. The most indiscriminate. The most theatrical. The most catalysing. And, probably, the ones penetrating public psyche the most. Because, perhaps more than other types of terrorism, jihadist terrorism despises life's sacredness. Because, perhaps more than other types of terrorism, it wants to strike values and every aspect of the daily physical and psychological sphere, making no distinctions.

And probably because jihadism seems to hover over our lives. It enters households through the news. It becomes a crucial element in the political debate on security. It increases suspicion over Muslims and Muslim immigrants. It accompanies us whenever we go to airports, train stations, and subways. It even mirrors itself in the guns of officers guarding public sites and piazzas, and in peoples' frightened looks. Simply put, a radicalised bomber might always be an arm away, striking any moment, just like in Paris, London, Brussels, Berlin, Barcelona, or Stockholm.

Unsurprisingly, jihadist radicalisation and terrorism incarnate very hot topics. For some, their threat is magnified by the media and certain politicians to mask racism and denied rights. For others, the kind of fear stemming from such phenomena is not socially constructed, but it is indeed existential and, hence, it requires strong countermeasures.

From whatever perspective one might approach them, radicalisation, terrorism and, in general, violence in the name of God surely remain truly controversial matters.

Especially within the Islamic community, people do not talk about such issues with pleasure.

Before embarking on the journey across the peninsula, a dear Imam warns me: "In this historical moment, after so many attacks, the community is afraid, Michele ... it is going to be hard". "You will not be able to talk about these things, for no one will talk, "reiterates a university colleague.

In fact, for the first few months, I only manage to collect a handful of numbers. On radicalisation and terrorism, a few people are willing to share their ideas. That is understandable. This is what could happen if I travelled to certain parts of Italy asking about Mafia, Camorra, and Ndrangheta. Some wouldn't want to talk about them. Many would be afraid. And a few others would not show their support publicly.

But as I walk in front of Giotto's bell tower in Florence, ISIS strikes Brussels. In the following months, attacks in numerous European cities take place one after the other. Radicalisation and terrorism turn into public matters. Within the societal debate, narratives become increasingly heated. Object of alarmism and unfair generalisations linking it to such heinous crimes, the Islamic community might be shutting its doors soon, I being to fear.

And yet, it is precisely at this point that dozens of Muslims feel the duty to share their views about radicalisation and terrorism.

The first interesting fact concerns the perception of radicalisation, here conceptualised as the support (and not participation) for violence in the name of God.

According to most examined Muslims, in general terms, Islam does not have a problem of radicalisation. In the surveys, 20% of the sample (86/440) thinks this issue might exist; otherwise, 44% (194/440) believe that radicalisation is minimal and exaggerated by the media, and 26% (115/440) believe it is not an issue at all. The absence of a true issue is even more noticeable when it comes to Islam in Italy. Only 10% of the sample (46/440) believes the Italian Islamic communities is actually afflicted by radicalisation; on the contrary, 30% (132/440) deem the question minimal and 43% (189/440) declare radicalisation is no issue at all.

This does not mean that the study's participants deny the existence of violence in the name of Islam. However, radicalisation would not be a problem because jihadists are not part of Islam in the first place. From north to south, 8 out of 10 respondents claim that: "He who commits atrocities is not a true Muslim"; "We do not consider terrorists to be brothers, for they are our enemies "; "Terrorists don't know what true Islam is, as they know nothing about religion in general"; "He who kills goes against the message of the Prophet and the wrath of Allah is upon him"; "Islam is a perfect religion and those who become radical stop being Muslim ... or perhaps they have never been true Muslims"; "There cannot be a problem of radicalisation in Islam because these people do not represent us, they are not part of our community, not here or anywhere in the world".

It is not surprising, therefore, that the vast majority of the Islamic community categorically rejects religious violence. 7 out of 10 participants (303/440) say that violence in the name of religion cannot be justified. 76% (334/440) repudiate Al Qaeda and 77% (338/440) ISIS. In the post-Charlie Hebdo era, almost 60% (271/440) declare they are against punishing those who offend Islam and its Prophet.

Such opposition to of all forms of violence in the name of God emerges impetuously in the interviews, where almost 9 out of 10 subjects (181/200) dismantle the terrorists' motifs.

First and foremost, interviewees stress jihadists' scriptural and theological ignorance. Ahmed, for example, explains the importance of interpreting and conceptualising sacred texts, such as the Koran, which end up being ignored, misunderstood and exploited by terrorists:

"Why do you mean when you say that terrorists do not follow the Koran?", I ask.

"Because you can't take a verse, a whole Surah, or whatever you want to read, and go kill someone That's not how the Koran works".

"Forgive my ignorance, how does the Koran work?".

"You must understand the historical period it was written in. At the time of Muhammad, peace be upon Him, we had to fight, first to survive, then to take back the Arab territories. That was what we call 'The Medina period'. But, from there on, we entered the 'Mecca period'. It is true, there have been so many wars, but it was the historical period that was so violent. Now, Islam has a house and you cannot kill the merciful name of Allah".

"What about those who do kill saying they do read and follow the Koran literally?".

"The Koran, as well as other verses from the Talmud and the Bible, says different things, which may seem contradictory. However, as it is for all things, we must understand the context, interpret, and adapt the challenges to today's world. Jihad is not the war against unbelievers in flesh and blood... Jihad is the war against the sin that is in each of us ... this is the real war".

Abdul and Umair also underline the end of the "Medina Period", undermining terrorists' doctrinal justifications: "When Islam was born, there were people who wanted to kill us and, at the time of Mohammed, in Medina, we had to survive; but now we haven't been in that period for so many centuries and the Koran teaches us to love and fight against sin", says Abdul. Along the same lines, Umair states that:" The time of fighting with the sword has ended ... now the struggle is within the soul, to be better believers ... it is no longer the Middle Ages, the Koran and the Prophet teach other things".

Regardless of the "Medina Period", jihadists still continue to break crucial scriptural tenets, argue Kafeel and Ghusun from Rome and Venice. As Kafeel explains, "one person cannot burn and kill plants, animals, houses, buildings ... in short, everything that terrorists do, that is, destroy and kill innocents, including women and children, is an insult to God, who instead even teaches you how to fight in the event that you are forced to go to war". "Even during battle", Ghusun articulates "if a Christian or a non-Muslim person surrenders and does not fight back, the Koran says you cannot kill him, but you must treat him well, you cannot torture him; therefore terrorists do not read the Koran, because they steal, rape, kill women and children and burn ... and last thing is especially forbidden, for only God can use fire!".

Having elucidated this, dozens of respondents wish to remind jihadists of Islam's peaceful nature. For Qirat, "Islam is a religion of peace; when we say goodbye, we say 'Salam', which means 'Peace', because a Muslim must always seek peace, otherwise he is not a Muslim". "Islam teaches us to love not only people, but all of the earth too, including all plants and living beings ", reiterates Aida, to the point that "if you are a true Muslim, you cannot even kill one ant without insulting God ", points out Wafi. In reality, "there is a verse of the Koran which says that if you kill one person, you kill all of humanity ... therefore, you see, the Koran orders us to live in peace ... perhaps the terrorists have forgotten to read this part", says Benazir.

The life of Prophet Muhammad is also mentioned as a tool of rejection of violence. Gazi recalls how the Prophet was "beaten, humiliated and abused, but He never asked Allah to kill people, for He actually prayed for them, for their health, and their prosperity". "There was a lady who every day emptied her garbage bin on the Prophet's house footsteps;

one day the Prophet saw that there was no dirt in front of His house and so He worried, for He didn't feel joy, and rushed to see the woman, asking her if she was well, showing her the kind of love that only God could give", tells Said. Likewise, Saadat emphasises that "people have insulted our Prophet all the time but he has never felt hatred; so, you understand that terrorists do the opposite of what the most important person did for us".

In this sense, dozens of interviewees restate this kind of rejection of violence in the name of God even when icons are disrespected. Though caricatures and cartoons can be offensive, most individuals feel violence is never the answer. "I don't like those who draw ugly caricatures and offend my religion ... but, one, we live in a free society; two, killing or hurting to people to prove they are wrong is a contradiction and is not even Islamic", proudly says Ish. "I can tell you that you are wrong and that it's not nice to insult another religion, but if you still decide to write dirty jokes, be my guest, you have every right to do so", reiterates Fadi. As Yar does:" We are all free to do what we want; one is free to write what he wants, just like I am free to say that what they write is wrong and offensive, but it must all end there, as do quarrels over football or politics".

In truth, for 23 respondents, those who offend Islam can actually be punished, but only through legal means. For instance, a Palestinian activist residing in Rome shows no hesitation as he affirms that whoever offends Muhammad "must [...] be immediately sued". In a similar manner, several second-generation students in Lombardy explain how:

"Muhammad cannot be touched, for He is too sacred for us. We agree with freedom of thought, but one's freedom ends when another person's freedom begins. We respect all the prophets, including Abraham, Moses, Jesus and even the Virgin Mary, because, if you don't, you can't be a true Muslim. Therefore, since we respect this, why can't people respect our Prophet and our sacred truth? This is when we can sue, if that happens". All of this, however, must be done peacefully, as Turkish workers clarify: "No one must be punished physically, but legally". "Even if you insult the Prophet, I cannot kill you... I can sue you, but, for Allah, I cannot use violence in His name and whoever does so is not a Muslim", two waiters in Milan repeat. For Arif, a Shiite, "if you insult Muhammad, I can rebuke you verbally... for us, that is already a form of great punishment ... no need for violence, as you see".

On that note, others invite terrorists to live by the Koran's peaceful teachings wherever they are. A Moroccan seller from Brescia shares this with me:

"You know, we came here many years ago. It wasn't always easy. At first, we missed home and people didn't treat us well. But we didn't get discouraged, we stayed strong and tried to do what the Koran says. The Koran tells us that us Muslims must be like a tree wherever we are, whether we live in a Muslim Arab country or in a Christian country; we must be planted, grow and bear fruit. If people do not love us, then it means that we are not making Allah happy.Us Muslims can't hurt others and we can't behave badly either... we have to be like a tree and show that there is something good at the base. Now I ask you: do trees misbehave? Do they shoot at you when you're in a bar with your friends? So, what's behind terrorism? Good or evil?".

At this point, it does not really surprise me that a few interviewees show anger and resentment towards jihadists. According to Jawad, Al Qaeda, ISIS and "all those who kill in the name of God are Islam's shame, just as Mafia is a pile of shit for most Italians". "Al Qaeda and ISIS? They are bastards, dogs, sacks of shit", proclaim Jundub and Ejaz. Lamis' comments are also eloquent:

"It makes me laugh when they tell us that we support these people. Guys, haven't you understood that yet? We wholeheartedly hate these sons of bitches. They are crazy and bastards, and they make us live bad…they say they defend Islam, but they don't know Islam. They should go fuck themselves! We are the first victims of this so-called 'Islamic' terrorism, remember!".

This is a good exhortation. As a terrorism scholar, I often forget about it. Terrorism does not strike Westerners only, for it affects all of us.

In reality, jihadist terrorism kills more Muslims than non-Muslims, precisely because the latter are considered apostates - "if you do not agree with the vision of Islam I believe in, I'll kill you", so to speak. And while this happens in the deafening silence of Western media, such criminal actions obscure entire communities, nullify years of hard work and integration, betray those values that younger generations try to internalise daily, creating labels and marginalisation.

In this regard, Rabi's testimony, from Catania, is touching. It shows what terrorism can take away from so young peoples' lives.

It's one of those ridiculously hot days in Sicily - when you can hardly breathe. Reminding myself to be in Catania, I decide to go for a cold granita. Finally, I find a kiosk that sells them. After I buy one I end up setting next to this big muscular, longhaired guy. As we start chatting, Rabi asks why on Earth I find myself sitting there on such a warm day. As I begin to explain the reasons for my visit, Rabi starts sharing his inner pain with disarming genuineness:

"I hate ISIS. Nobody can think good things about this madness. Nobody can tell me what terrorism is," he says resolutely.

"How so?".

"Because I know it. I know what terrorism means. Two of my best friends left Tunisia and died in Syria, deceived by ISIS".

"Did you get to talk to them before they left?".

"I ..." Rabi stops with tears in his eyes. "Yes, I did, but that didn't help and now they are dead".

"May I ask you, how are you feeling?"

"I feel so much pain... you can't die at age twenty-five for something criminal, which goes against everything they taught us as children and everything that Allah says. You know, my friends' mother, who is also kind of my mom, when she learned her children died, got sick and died a few days later? And for what? What the fuck!".

"Why do you think they left?".

"Because those bastards brainwashed thousands of people. They betrayed Islam, betrayed their parents, their families, turned their backs on their God, chasing bullshit".

"Bullshit?"

"Yes, money, whores, fame ... masked as serving God. How many died, taking my friends with them? You should have seen them, there was no way to make them snap out of it... this is what terrorism does...it lies to you; it kills you and, if you stay alive, it kills you inside".

Once again, it is difficult to remain numb. Rabi is a man of passion; I can look in his eyes and in the way he moves his hands. Rabi is angry. Wounded. Embittered. Disappointed And, above all, betrayed by those who took away his friends and made his friends' mother sick. Betrayed by those who, claiming to be Muslim, commit atrocities in the name of the same God he also believes in.

Dramatic, Rabi's words embody the sentiment by the overwhelming majority of the Islamic community, which goes against all forms of violence and the exploitation of religion for political ends.

But, unfortunately, not all participants think like Rabi.

Although 7 out of 10 subjects condemn violence in the name of God, a substantial minority of the sample, on the other hand, exalts it. In the surveys, individuals strongly or somehow agreeing with the justification of violence in defence of Islam amount to 24% (105/440).

Understandably, this attitude emerges more in anonymous written questionnaires rather than in the interviews, which tend to be more prudent. Nevertheless, 32 out of 200 respondents (15%), verbally express their support for violence framed in religious terms.

A number of individuals identify self-defence as the main motif that can justify violence in the name of Allah. "The only thing Islam allows for is self-defence, that is, if you are attacked, you can react. But offensive violence is never justifiable", three North African citizens from Bologna explain. In truth, in the words of a craftsman from Gambia in Verona, "only if there is a good cause can God allow [for violence], that is when you are forced to defend yourself".

Likewise, other participants accept violence in the name of God only vis-à-vis oppression. As an Egyptian entrepreneur in Milan reveals, "Islam and violence cannot go in the same sentence, unless you are talking about non- Muslims oppressing Muslims". In fact, as two Pakistani shopkeepers say, it would be a "natural [...] reaction to rebel and do everything you can to end oppression, even through force". Along the same lines, a young man from Bangladesh living in the Roman Torpagnattara district points out that "the only case in which violence is right is when there is oppression. Let's say that someone kills or attacks your family or your Muslim brothers, then you can attack or kill your enemy's family, because this is allowed by the Koran".

In support for violence, these are some of the most common expressions and comments that I hear during my journey from north to south: "If a brother is in danger and asks for help, I must go and help him if I want to be a good Muslim"; "If a brother is under the yoke of the oppressor, it is a religious duty to go help him"; "If there is oppression you are obliged to go and defend your Muslim brothers".

Countering what was mentioned to earlier, a considerable minority does support the duty to punish whoever offends Islam and its Prophet. Out of 440 subjects, those strongly accepting punishment of offenders' amount to 30% (131/440).

While the intention to punish who ever insults Islam does automatically imply the use of force, it is clear that respect for religious icons is a truly slippery topic. It is perhaps not so surprising that, despite the majority of respondents firmly condemn violence of all kinds, some show sympathy towards those who would react violently if Muhammad were offended. For example, a Tunisian student from Bologna predicts how the world "[...] is inevitably destined to wars of religion, because people do not understand offending Muhammad is that wrong". This type of sensitivity is also shared by a group of friends from Brescia, according to whom:

"You can insult me, my wife, my children and all the people who are here in front of you. You can insult us all, mock, and treat us badly from today until tomorrow and 100 days later. Obviously, that would hurt, but it wouldn't hurt much as if you offended our Prophet… all our lives, compared to Him, are worth nothing and, hence, when someone insults Muhammad, it hurts deep in our souls, for He is more sacred than our lives, for He is the dearest thing we nourish".

In light of such statements, 47 out of 200 people (about 25%) declare that anyone who insults Islam and its sacred principles deserves to be punished. This time, however, not everyone means through legal terms, as I understand during a conversation with a Moroccan mother behind a bakery in Verona. Sweet and polite, once we touch upon the matter of icons, the woman turns into another person. Her tone changes, as do her eyes, which are filled with anger: "Whoever offends Islam must be punished … severely and brutally ", the woman states, justifying, directly or not, the use of force.

Let me be clear. Expressing one's dissent with impetus does not automatically lead to violence. In general, how many people talk "big" and never make that transition to violence? Besides, those who never lose their cool and have bad thoughts, please raise your hand.

But the kind of remarks by 24 individuals backing the abovementioned Moroccan mother's view leave me troubled: "A person must be punished, even physically if that individual does not stop and repent"; "It is absolutely right to punish those who make fun of the Prophet, perhaps even physically, especially if that person continues to do so"; "I can't kill you, but I understand if someone punches you because you can't touch the Prophet". In the words of a Pakistani family man:

"Killing someone is out of the question. But, at the same time, as you have to discipline your children and punish them if they keep making mistakes, you have to do the same in this situation. If you decide to write offensive caricatures on Muhammad and I tell you that this insults me once, twice, three, four times etc, then maybe, if I give you a slap and then a punch, maybe you will stop it".

The rest of those who agree with the duty to punish offenders also emphasise the offenders' own stupidity. To them, given the amount of crazy and irascible people in the world, it would be unwise to insult Muhammad. In simple words, according to these participants, it's your fault if you offend the Prophet and you get hurt. Amongst the remarks that indirectly accept violence, the most explicit ones are: "If you decide to insult Muhammad, it is your risk, you should not do it"; "There are many crazy people and if you decide to provoke them, it is a risk you run, because now by now you should know how wrong it is to insult the Prophet"; "It is wrong to kill people, but, if you insult Muhammad and you then have to deal with hot heads, it is your fault".

Furthermore, 10% of the sample (44/440) supports Al Qaeda's struggle, and supporters of ISIS amount to 13% (57/440).

Once again, these estimates are predictably greater in the written questionnaires than in the interviews. In fact, only 7 out of 200 people (3.5% of the total) openly show their support for the two terrorist organisations.

Again, the main reasons to support such organisations seems to be the failure or inability to defend Muslim citizens, resulting into the alleged subsequent religious duty to combat oppression. In the words of a group of North African workers in Reggio Emilia:

"Imagine you are a Syrian citizen now. They bomb you all day long. Your house is destroyed and there is nothing left for you, except for destruction and death. Who will come protect you? Assad? Putin? The West? No, only other true Muslims who are obliged to come protect you if you are in danger. If there is violence, if people are dying and the West does nothing, what is left for the Syrians to do? If other people don't want to intervene, only death awaits the Syrians. You see that, at this point, it is really a religious duty for every true Muslim to go and defend oppressed and persecuted brothers".

In a similar fashion, a Senegalese seller from Naples talks against Bashir Assad and the West, depicting Al Qaeda and ISIS as "the [...] only defenders of the oppressed people of Syria and the Middle East", who are martyred "by the Syrian and Western regimes that massacre them every day", a Somali worker repeats, because "If it were not for them [Al Qaeda and ISIS]", the man continues, "there would be much more blood in that area".

I repeat. It is crucial to point out that the vast majority of individuals repudiate violence in the name of Allah, Qaeda and ISIS. Nevertheless, it is equally important to emphasise that a smaller but significant percentage of the sample supports violence exactly framed in religious terms. For these people, if someone insults or attacks Islam and Muslims, it is a duty of every true believer to protect oppressed brothers.

These findings could be troublesome for two reasons. The first concerns numbers. While they are the minority within the sample, 105 individuals who still believe that violence in the name of God can be justified cannot be defined as a low number. Considering what happened at Charlie Hebdo, 131 individuals agreeing with the need to punish offenders is not a low number. Neither are 44 and 53, respectively supporting

Al Qaeda and ISIS – even though these numbers are definitely inferior when compared to other European countries.

The second source of worry is perhaps even more puzzling, however. As previously illustrated, perception of radicalization within the Italian Muslim community is minimal. For Italian Muslims, radicalisation is not be a true issue.

It's true. At least initially, no alcoholic claims to have a problem with alcohol. Thus, no radicalised person admits that he has become radicalised. And, besides, people might not even be willing to admit they have a problem in the first place–just like some Italians might feel shame or fear in identifying infiltrations by Mafia Camorra and 'Ndrangheta.

However, considering that we are not in Kashmir, the Palestinian Territories, or Chechnya, it is natural to expect low rates of support for religious violence, along with a more grounder (and maybe sincere) perception by the community. I fear that, in one way or the other, these findings indicate that the Islamic community does not fully know what happens within its boundaries. Islamist violent radical visions exist. And these cannot be labelled marginal, even if we are in Italy.

That asserted, I can't help but interrogate myself as to which factors might fuel the acceptance of violence in the name of Allah. Is it about denied rights and discrimination? Lack of social and economic equal opportunities? Personal traumatic experiences? Or is there something else?

In order to shed light upon the possible reasons for supporting violence, I ask participants what they themselves think are the drivers of radicalization. The first five factors selected are the following:

1) Exploitation of Islam for political purposes (chosen 13% of the time amongst the first 3 drivers);

2) Material and spiritual benefits offered by Al Qaeda and ISIS (nominated in 12% of cases);

3) Lack of a strong debate within Islam (11%);

4) Personal traumatic experiences (9.4%);

5) Economic and social hardship (8.4%)

Among the other causes we identify, in order: identity crises affecting individuals trapped between the Muslim worlds and Western cultures; oppression by Arab governments; denied rights; Western racism; outrage at Western foreign policy; personal contacts with extremists; the Israeli-Palestinian conflict; search for adventure; the call to arms for every true Muslim.

Two hundred pages of statistical analysis contradict, however, the participants' perceptions. Neither the "usual suspects" nor the factors identified by Italian Muslims explain support for violence. Statistical tests also exclude theories of discrimination, racism (and Islamophobia), economic disparity, outrage at Western foreign policy, and oppression of Muslims in the world.

In the same way, I do not report any significant connection between material and spiritual benefits and support for violence in the name of God. Even traumatic experiences and personal contacts with extremists are not as important. And no "classical" sociological variables, including sex, age, nationality, religious orientation, education, economic status, etc., is ultimately relevant.

Although identity crises and difficulties at the workplace are marginally associated with support of force, what really influences certain individuals' potentially violent opinions is precisely their Islamist vision. This is captured within the two main the ideological variables of the study: sacredness of religious icons and support for a theocratic government centred on Islamic law (Sharia).

Let's start with the first variable. In the study, those who would punish anyone who offends Islam and its Prophet are also significantly more likely to justify violence in the name of Allah, Al Qaeda and ISIS. This fact is crucial, because, as already explained, punishment is not synonymous for violence. If insulted, a person may sue offenders without any use of force.

If, however, within the surveys, those who take offense are also the ones who are most likely to support violence, there is a chance these people do not purely see "punishment" through "legal means", but also through physical violence. Obviously, we cannot know for sure, considering the fact that anonymous questionnaires might have facilitated this, doubts are legitimate.

Concretely, out of 105 people agreeing with the duty to punish offenders, 82 also accept violence in defence of the faith. On the contrary, out of 283 individuals opposed to punishing offenders, only 46 support the use of force. In statistical terms, the difference between the two groups (4: 1 ratio in favour of violence and 1: 5 against violence) is enormous. Not surprisingly, the probability that a subject who accepts to punish offenders of Islam also justifies violence in the name of God is almost 80%. This result reflects, by far, the strongest relationship between two variables in the entire study.

As already mentioned, the second variable that is most associated to justification of violence is support for a theocratic government and the belief that the latter is better than a democracy. In other words, within the study, those who believe in a Sharia-based government are considerably more inclined to justify the use of force in the name of Allah, Al Qaeda and ISIS than those who do not share the same vision –displaying more than a 60%probability to accept violence.

In light of these data, several clarifications are due. Firstly, these results do not automatically link Islam and violence. Nor do they necessarily associate Islamist visions with support and use of force. In reality, the vast majority of Islamists do not use violence and do not even justify it. Let us remember: the process of interpretation and internalisation of sacred texts is a highly subjective and intimate matter.

What these data reveal, however, is that, within this study, Islamist visions are crucial at shaping certain answers. In this context, the difference between those who support Islamist visions and those who do not is striking.

That asserted, another aspect I would like to discuss is anti-Israeli sentiment. This is not naturally associated to violence in defence of faith and may perhaps be considered peripheral in the debate on radicalisation in Italy. In addition, the Israeli-Palestinian conflict is one of the most complex issues in international politics. It is often highly politicised and polarises discussions in Europe, the Middle East, and the rest of the world.

Still, similarly to the already mentioned anti-Semitic conspiracy theories, the study is once again affected by attitudes and ideas that resonate hatred.

Certainly, the fact that virtually every examined subject shows sympathy for the Palestinian people is somehow granted. Likewise, the fact that the vast majority of the Muslim community feels critical of the Israeli government is also understandable – even Israeli society itself is profoundly divided on heated matters such as the peace process with the

Palestinians. Criticism, perplexity, and doubt are legitimate. Especially if one takes into account a number of Israeli military operations and proportionality issues. The issue of Jerusalem. Water. Status and return of Palestinian refugees. Disputed borders. Settlements. The vision of a viable Palestinian state. Decades of conflict and unsolved dilemmas can't avoid harsh criticism, on either side.

But when the right to existence of a nation is denied, wishing for its death and destruction, one crosses the line.

In the survey, 52% of the sample (230/440) states Israel has no right to exist. In the interviews, more than 6 out of 10 people (122/200) reiterate this sentiment. From north to south, the most recurrent phrases deal with the expulsion of Israelis not only from settlements in the West Bank, but from the entire nation of Israel: "Those bastard dogs have to leave!"; "Sooner or later, the Israelis will be thrown back into the sea"; "They stole the land as the Americans did with Native Americans, but, soon, the Palestinians will come back and kick the Jews' ass"; "The land belongs to the Palestinians and to Allah, whose anger is upon the Jews, who will then be defeated and driven from Jerusalem and all the cities"; "Europe has created Israel, but it is time for the Israelis to return to Poland, Slovakia, Spain and France, for they have no right to stay there"; "The Jews have never been in the Middle East, Jesus Christ was Palestinian and the Israelis are like the Nazis, but just like them, they will die and the earth will return Muslim".

Though insulting, such statements and distorted visions of history (Jesus Christ was Jewish and the term "Palestine" was coined to eradicate the Jewish presence after the Roman destruction of the Temple of Jerusalem), may not be taken too seriously. But they start becoming worrisome the instant they undermine what the international community has been working for years: the creation of two states for two people, one Palestinian and one Israeli.

Now, as we've said, whilst criticising complex issues is legitimate, denying Israel's right to exist is just not admissible. First, it hinders Palestinian calls to self-determination. How can people tell Israelis they have no right to exist and live where they were born when the Palestinians seek the same thing? Furthermore, denying Israel's right to exist destroys any peace proposal between the two parties, which Italy and its diplomatic missions have been continuously advocating for. In other words, peace is not unilateral. It takes two to make it and rejecting one of the two elements of the equation is not peace, but something else.

Not surprisingly, almost half of the sample (49%, 215/440) does not consider Hamas and Hezbollah as terrorist groups. In the interviews, the same subjects who deny Israel's right to exist often support the two organisations despite their patent goal (as spelled in their manifesto) is the destruction of Israel. And it's not just that. In dozens of cases, members of Hamas and Hezbollah are even idolised and revered: "They are the defenders of the Palestinian people, holy warriors who will go to Heaven with Allah"; "They are angels that God sent to protect the Palestinians"; "We all respect them because they fight for freedom against an occupying force, it is not terrorism, but resistance"; "We pray for them to be able to defeat as many Israelis as possible, take back Jerusalem, and make all Palestinians return home"; "Besides Messi and Cristiano Ronaldo, they are the real heroes who sacrifice their lives for something greater, for freedom, for Israel and the Jews cannot enslave us".

These remarks are problematic for two reasons. To begin with, they go against what the European Union declares, highlighting diametrical views and attitudes.

Brussels labels both Hamas and Hezbollah (at least its military wing) terrorist organisations, just like Al Qaeda and ISIS, even though they differ. Hezbollah and, above all, Hamas are fighting for a nationalist cause linked to a specific territory and reality. Hence, it is no surprise that their struggle is considered by many as resistance carried out by freedom fighters. If one looks at the end and at the reasons for armed struggle, the same subjects will always be defined as terrorists by some and as liberators by others. But if one starts looking at the *way* and at *how* you decide to fight, then the difference could be starker.

It's true. There is no official, recognised definition of terrorism, but one of its major components is the targeting of civilians. Obviously, it's not black and white. States can do the same harm terrorists do. Sadly, the Israeli Defence Force (IDF) has killed and continues to kill Palestinian civilians, including women and children. These actions, however, in addition to being analysed and judged by domestic courts, are not systematically strategized and executed as military tactics. And in Israel, at least on paper, whoever makes mistakes can pay. There have been and are exceptions, but generally speaking, that is what can happen. By contrast, to Hamas and Hezbollah, there are no "real" civilians in Israel. And this is precisely the point. The calculated use of terrorist tactics against unarmed civilians, through suicide attacks, bus bombing, kidnappings, torture, and the indiscriminate firing of rockets, is also what has pushed the EU to label Hamas and Hezbollah terrorist organisations.

Thus, not only does the unwillingness by many participants to call these group "terrorists" betray the very idea of civilians being innocent and untouchable; it also undermines everything that I've heard against violence in the name of God.

Let us remember. "Hezbollah" means "Party of God". While they are fighting for the Palestinian cause, both Hezbollah and Hamas justify their actions in religious terms. Contrary to "classical" past Palestinian groups, made of communists and nationalists, the two organisations fight, as they themselves state, to defend Islam too. They revere martyrdom. As martyrs, they believe to go to Heaven where 70 virgins await them. They repudiate any secular vision. In principle, they reject man-made peace agreements, granting no compromise with infidels. They fight, kill, and die for Allah.

Bluntly, Hamas and Hezbollah are, by definition, the justification of violence in the name of God. And, as for this aspect, they do not substantially differ from Al Qaeda and ISIS.

Yet, at least in 60% of the interviews, this does not seem to matter much, for the kind of resentment towards Israelis can justify the same violence that had been loudly repudiated minutes before.

Maybe my conversation with this group of students in Lombardy can best summarise what I've just said.

I've been chatting to them for a while and I am thrilled. These young men before me are just good. They joyfully share all kinds of information with me, opening their hearts. They are smart, well-spoken, and respectful. Their enthusiasm inspires me, especially as they offer me an almost endless list of reasons according to which in no case can one kill in the name of God. They mention how even smashing a fly is against Islam. They recite every verse and Surah from the Koran that condemns the use of force. They say that terrorists are fake Muslims, for they are shameful beings hurting the name of Muhammad. And they all say they hate ISIS.

I couldn't be happier!

But when we come to the subject of Hamas and Israel, tone changes. The latter becomes aggressive. Hostility is palpable. Three guys jump in saying members of Hamas are not terrorists. A bit perplex and intrigued, I ask them to explain to me what why they think so:

"So guys, why is ISIS a terrorist organisation while Hamas is not?", I ask.

"Because Hamas fights for freedom"

"But they also justify violence in the name of God," I reply.

"Yes, but their cause is holy…just".

"But haven't you just told me that there are no cases in which one can kill for Allah, for killing is always wrong?".

"But that is different".

"How so?".

"There you fight for the land, for your people, because Israel kills women and children and they will never stop. They are the terrorists. So, it is different, and, in this situation, you can fight".

"But, defending yourself in one thing, while starting hostilities is another thing. So, is it okay if many Israelis die?".

"Of course. They kill the Palestinians; the Palestinians strike back".

"Okay, I get that, but what about when members of Hamas sneak into an Israeli house and brutally stab and murder every member of the family, including the children, when they are still in bed sleeping; isn't that terrorism?".

"They bomb you; you respond. Everyone fights with the tools they have".

"Okay, bear with me. If an Israeli pilot bombs Gaza and kills, not Hamas soldiers, who Israel is at war with, but many helpless and innocent women and children: what is this person?".

"A terrorist".

"According to what you have previously told me today, if the Israeli soldier is a terrorist, what's a Hamas member blowing himself up on a bus killing as many people as possible, including defenceless women and children, who are not wearing an IDF uniform?".

"But that is the thing, there are no civilians in Israel. They all are in the army; if they don't fight you today, they'll do it tomorrow".

Do you know what troubles me the most? It's not the fact that the students contradict themselves challenging the case they had made against violence in the name of God minutes before.

These young men are all university students. They were born in Italy. They study political science. Medicine. Engineering. Languages. They have never been to Israel or the Palestinian territories. I am pretty sure that none of them kwon one single Palestinian, one single Israeli, or even one single Jewish person.

Besides, they have nothing to do with the Palestinian cause, per se. They are not Palestinian citizens. Like me, they do not know what it means to be at war. Like me, they do not know what it feels like.

And yet, the instant we address the Israeli-Palestinian conflict, the students completely flipflop. As they hear the word "Israel", I am not able to reason with them any longer, which, let's be careful, it does not mean changing their mind. Rather, it means the ability to analyse situations a bit more critically and impartially, as universities try to teach. *This* is the thing that I most regret. And I can't really understand why.

There is no doubt: empathy is a noble thing. But completely ignoring what had been strongly labelled wrong minutes before, that is, the justification of violence in the name of God, is just puzzling to me. "All of Palestine, and I mean everything, is Muslim land, holy to us, where a Jewish nation cannot exist", an activist tells me a few days later in Rome. Can this be the ultimate reason then?

I have no answer to this question.

But one thing appears clear. Unfortunately, in a way or the other, for most of the Muslim community, Israel triggers contrasting feelings. It seems that this matter is even more controversial than terrorism, for Israel often embodies the exception that can justify violence in the name of God. And this is alarming. Given our recent history. Given our diplomatic, economic, and cultural relations with Tel Aviv. Given the arduous peace process. And given the kind of society we try to be. Such anti-Israeli feelings cannot be underestimated.

At this point, however, it is worth mentioning that not all respondents show hatred towards Israel. Some individuals living outside Rome and Milan, for instance, just have no interest in what is happening there. Others admit they know very little about the whole question: "Look, I only think about myself and work, for I have so many problems that I don't really know what is going on over there"; "I am not interested in politics, which always causes problems"; "I do not care"; "I don't know much, and I only care about my job"; "I don't know anyone from there and so in my family we never talk about it... maybe when something happens, but for us it's not a problem".

Other individuals are not afraid of defining Hamas and Hezbollah as terrorist groups. Short but intense is Hazim's testimony:

"Hamas, Hezbollah, ISIS, Al Qaeda ... they all ruin the Arab Muslim world. They are scum, for they are terrorists...and this is precisely because they are barbaric people, who can only act violently. They are criminals who should be put in jail. And I am sorry, because, especially in the Palestinian case, Hamas and Hezbollah prevent peace with Israel, which is a great nation all Muslims have to learn from. In Israel, Jews and Muslims actually live in peace. Gaza, instead, is controlled by Hamas, which is like Mafia...for shame!".

Similarly, Misbah, from Turin, declares that anyone who acts violently "is not a Muslim and [for this] so many Palestinians are wrong". To Riyadh, "the Palestinians are a great people, as are Jews and Israelis, but they both must fight the terrorists who hold both Palestine and Israel hostage". "Hamas and Hezbollah are terrorists, just as ISIS and Al Qaeda are, for they all know nothing about the Koran", concludes Ridha.

On a couple of occasions, I even meet people who understand Israel's need for a nation the Jewish people can call home. "After all they have been through, they too have the right to live in the Middle East. It is true, there have been wars with the local inhabitants, but now everyone has the right to stay there, including Israel", says Deeba. As does Ulfat: "The Jews have been persecuted and they too want to live in peace; they too come from there, Jews and Muslims are cousins, so I don't see the reason why Israel should not exist and why they can't all live in peace".

Other respondents still criticise Israel, but argue responsibilities are to be allocated to both sides. "Israel must apologise for what it has done; however, Hamas should also do so", proposes Idris. "Israel should leave the occupied territories, but every non-Muslim person must feel at ease in Palestine and, in this, Hamas is wrong, for it is only a violent and mafia-like organisation that cannot represent the Palestinians", thunders Ghayur. To Ibn, "All of them, I mean Hamas and Hezbollah, are terrorists and, as long as they continue to fire missiles, the Israeli government can always wage war and continue its occupation ... see, it's really these organisations that ruin Palestine".

In this respect, I find this young student's reflection to be enlightening:

"As I was filling out your questionnaire with my friends, we reached the question on Hamas and Hezbollah. Everybody started saying they are not terrorists, voicing their hatred of Israel. But this is so wrong! Especially if we call ourselves Muslims, we must bring peace. Israel does wrong things, but it is made up of people like us. They too have a heart, and so the members of Hamas. But they both are wrong and, since we live here, far away, we have the responsibility to bring them together, so they can get to know each other and toss their weapons. We can't wish for Israel's destruction. Dialogue is the only way to solve problems…only if Jews and Palestinians start talking to each other again can things improve. But if we, being the ones living here in peace, keep hating Israel, we cannot help our beloved Palestinians".

Equally to anti-Semitism, anti-Israeli sentiment is also a source of concern. Reflections like the ones by the above mentioned student are a good starting point, but often remain isolated. That is why, as we'll see shortly, both the Italian society and the Muslim community have to do their part. The aim is not just to address anti-Semitic feelings that are still vivid in our memory; it also to clarify, once and for all, the matter of violence in the name of God. Even if the latter seems a pretty black and white choice, my journey across the peninsula teaches me it's not always so simple.

The Journey and the Meeting of Two Worlds

After multiple intense experiences and encounters, I can finally say that it's the end of the line. So, what are the main takeaways after this journey inside the Italian Muslim community? How could we summarise everything we have seen so far?

Well, as for racism, discrimination and Islamophobia, we can say that the community is divided into two blocks. The first, which a bit more than half of the sample, is composed of those individuals who, as Muslims, feel discriminated against. For these people, life's not easy. Racist and Islamophobic attitudes characterise their experience at school, at work, and at a number of public venues. As such, they feel incapable of expressing their faith freely, as many struggle at obtaining permits for larger places of worship. Their different outfits and traditions can become source of embarrassment and unease. Accused of supporting terrorism and contributing to the loss of Italian identity, these people feel crushed by such veiled and subtle assumptions. On top of it, they feel demonised by the media and certain politicians, who, in turn, construct a "Muslim question" to earn money, win elections, and satisfy international agendas. In the end, these people are often frustrated, because, for them, being Muslim in Italy is a fundamentally problematic choice.

By contrast, the second block knows no discrimination or racism. For these individuals, life in Italy is substantially devoid of any major hardship linked to Islamic identity. They benefit from traditional Italian kindness and hospitality. They do not perceive the kind of racism and Islamophobia they hear about. They don't get shadowed by the jihadist threat, nor by the weight of Italian culture, for their Muslim identity doesn't seem to have a negative impact on the various facets of everyday life. They have no difficulty blending in at school or at the workplace. The don't feel betrayed by the system, for they are grateful to be able to pray freely. And they don't care much about the media either, for they know the media don't represent all of Italy. In the end, for these people, racism, discrimination, and Islamophobia remain unknown concepts.

In terms of integration, first impression might tell us a tale of success. In the surveys, 81% of the sample declares to love Italy and wants to be part of its culture. But, while this percentage sounds like a hymn to integration, the interviews offer a more complex picture. If by "integration" we mean the search for balance and common ground, the community appears once again divided. On the one hand, one can't help but bask in the type of passionate enthusiasm and gratitude people like Mimmo and Kamal show, feeling pride in their dual Italian and Muslim identity. On the other hand, one is struck by homophobic, sexist, absolutist, conspiracist, anti-Western, anti-Christian, and anti-Semitic sentiments, which are just incompatible with those values younger generations try to internalise so bad.

Women, second generations, and converts all offer a rich and variegated mosaic of the Italian Islamic community. Although I am still fairly convinced that many are satisfied with life in general, the Muslim women I interact with cannot help but share their discomfort. On one side, this is directly connected to their aesthetic appearance (veil, burka) and the subsequent embarrassment and / or impossibility to publicly manifest one's religious beliefs. On the other side, discomfort is not related to mainstream society, but, rather, to the Muslim community itself, which often meets demands for greater emancipation with sexist and chauvinist demeanours. What strikes me the most, however, is the kind of strength I see in most of these women, as they fight for their right to religious freedom or emancipation. They suffer, but, as gently as possible, they don't give up.

Second generations are simply impetuous. Usually, they are really proactive and constructive. They appreciate current challenges affecting both Italy and the Islamic community, realising their help is much needed. Hence, they don't sit around. They think. They act. They build cultural, social, and economic bridges. They apply their energies to find their position in the country they love passionately. Why? Because these young people feel Italian.

And yet, even amongst those who were born in Italy, while a minority, we encounter subjects who are incompatible with our country. Sadly, these stand out, for not only do they hate other groups, but they even promote total rejection and replacement of Italian traditions and shared values. If not addressed, such dissonant voices could obstruct the type of potentially extraordinary journey many of their peers have already embarked upon.

Though a minority within the study, Italian converts also act as glue between society and the Muslim community. Culturally active, converts feel responsible to facilitate the Muslim's community's integration process and its ever-so-sought official entente with the Italian State. However, once again, instances of hatred towards Italian and Christian values emerge, coupled with patent attempts to Islamise Italy from within. As for second generations, if ignored, such visions could undermine genuine and constructive attempts to build cultural bridges and increase social cohesion.

Now, onto radicalisation, terrorism and violence in the name of God. To begin with, most Italian Muslims do not believe that there is a problem of radicalisation within Islam or within the Italian Islamic community. This is because, first and foremost, terrorists would not be part of Islam, for they are identified as criminals who ignore and exploit certain theological aspects for vile purposes. Not surprisingly, the vast majority of participants categorically rejects violence in defence of faith, the duty to punish those who offend Islam and its Prophet, and the struggle by both Al Qaeda and ISIS.

Nevertheless, not only does a substantial but significant minority accept force in defence of Islam, but it also motivates violence precisely in religious terms. For these people, it would be every Muslim's duty to fight oppression of Muslim brethren. This is the reason why these individuals actually praise and glorify Al Qaeda and ISIS, who are believed to be the defenders of faith and the oppressed. Interestingly, what really fuels violent visions is the obligation to defend the image and reputation of the Prophet Mohammed. To a substantial minority, regardless of Charlie Hebdo' stragic events, if sacred icons are insulted, force can be understood and justified, for it is every true believer's duty.

On a closer analytical look, the statistical analysis shows ideological visions to have the most impact for the justification of violence. No sociological factor normally associated to the acquisition of extreme and violent behaviours (poverty, discrimination, racism, resentment at the western foreign policy, oppression, etc.) is, in the end, statistically relevant. What really counts is, instead, the sensitive issue of the sacredness of religious icons and the preference of a theocratic government over a democratic one. This does not automatically link Islam or Islamist visions to violence. But the results do show that, within this study, those who support more literal visions of Islam (dealing with Muhammad's figure and Islamic law) are statistically more likely to accept violence framed in religious terms.

Finally, the majority of the community says that Israel has no right to exist and that Hamas and Hezbollah are not terrorist organisations. Contradicting the European Union's official position, most of the sample considers the members of such groups as freedom fighters. While the Israeli-Palestinian conflict remains one of the most intricate issues of international security (featuring major pieces of criticism aimed at Israel), not only do these visions contradict the type of narrative against terrorism that has been strongly supported throughout almost all of the study; they also betray the right to self-determination of a people and, with it, the peace process, for which Italy and the international community have been working for years. And the resulting degree of anti-Israeli and anti-Semitic sentiment, given our recent history, requires immediate attention.

Italian Muslims and Italian Non-Muslims

Before the conclusion, I think it is interesting to ask what the other element of this great equation thinks: the non-Muslim Italian society.

As specified in the introduction, this study displays no interviews by Italian non-Muslim citizens - being the emphasis on the opinions and attitudes of our fellow Muslim citizens. However, a similar survey carried out at the same time I was studying the Muslim community can still provide us with invaluable food for thought.

To being with, in regard to Muslims' social conditions, Italian non-Muslims do not think there is much racism or discrimination happening in Italy. For example, non-Muslim participants who agree with the claim that Italian Muslims have a hard time blending in at school and find a good job and a proper place of worship never amount to more than 20% (out of 440 subjects). While almost 40% (172/440) do admit that there is a sort of discrimination against Muslim citizens, "only" 43% state that there is a media war against Islam. In regard to these aspects, we have seen that the overwhelmingly majority of the examined Muslim citizens truly begs to differ.

In truth, the non-Muslim survey reveals a certain degree of hostility aimed at Muslims. Almost 48% of the sample (211/440) states that Islam and Italy are incompatible. 51% of the participants (223 / 440) do not believe that Muslims really love Italy. 41% (181/440) would never live in neighbourhood predominantly inhabited by Muslims. And, not surprisingly, 40% (178/440) believe that Islam represents a threat to our country.

In a way, these figures 81% of the Muslim sample (351/440) states, which is to love Italy and be part of it. In another way, these hostile numbers match equally worrisome visions by some members of the Islamic community openly rejecting Western habits and mixed marriages (respectively, 41% and 39% of the Muslim sample).

In terms of radicalisation and terrorism, the difference between the two groups' perceptions is considerable. Contrary to 20% of the Islamic community, 69% of non-Muslim subjects (304/440) deem radicalisation in Islam as a problem, even within the Italian context (44% versus 10%within the Muslim sample).

This perception gap conflicts with actual, empirical support for religiously framed violence Muslim participants display. Precisely, non-Muslim citizens who believe that, after all, Muslims do accept violence in the name of God are 172, while the surveys show that Muslims who think so are 105. Non-Muslims who believe that Muslims are likely to punish those who offend Islam and its Prophet are 188, while these amount to 131. And non-Muslims who believe that Muslims support Al Qaeda and ISIS are 120, while in the surveys the latter are 44 and 57. As we can observe, in every single case the perception of the threat is considerably greater than the actual empirical data from the questionnaires.

Nevertheless, when we compare the two groups' actual support for religious violence, Muslim participants always accept force more so than their non-Muslim counterparts.

Precisely, non-Muslims who accept violence in defence of faith number 40, while Muslims 105.Likewise, non-Muslims who would punish those who insult the sacredness of a religion and its icons amount to 68, whilst Muslims 131. Non-Muslims who agree with the struggle of Al Qaeda and ISIS are, respectively, 29 and 34; Muslims who support these groups amount to44 and 57. Though a minority, Muslims who accept violence always outnumber non-Muslim participants in every question that explores violence framed in religious terms. And lastly, while not strictly related to violence, Muslims who support anti-Israeli and anti-Semitic sentiments (backing Hamas, Hezbollah, and conspiracy theories) always outnumber their non-Muslim counterparts – constantly over 50% vs. 20%.

Finally, both groups see the future as mixture of uncertainty and hope. To some respect, non-Muslims seem to be more worried than their Muslim fellows. To 320 non-Muslims (73%), Italy will suffer a large jihadist terrorist attack, while the Muslims who think so are 119 (28%). Non-Muslims who believe that tension between Italian society and Islamic community will increase are 241 (55%); Muslims are 143 (32%).Still, both groups look at the future with hope, for 268 non-Muslims (61%) and 350 Muslims (80%) consider the integration of the Islamic community as an essential tool for a better tomorrow. Likewise, most Muslims and non-Muslims believe the key to a better future is multiculturalism (73% and 77%).

In light of all of this, are there any considerations and suggestions we can draw from this type of comparison? What emerges from this encounter? What should both Muslims and non-Muslims do?

Let's start from the non-Muslim respondents.

What I immediately realise and wish for is that non-Muslim citizens could show a bit more empathy, perhaps.

Let me be clear. I still believe Italy not to be a racist country. And the fact that almost half of the Muslim sample tells us they do not feel discriminated against is good. Notwithstanding, wrong perception about Islamic presence, habits, and beliefs might indicate fear and closure towards what is labelled different. Maybe we are not ready to accept and internalise the fact that we, as a nation, are changing too. That we are growing. That we are opening up to the world and, with it, to other cultures, stories and ways of life. But, sadly, for whatever reason, I spot more xenophobic visions than expected.

This kind of alleged fear is evident when it comes to the perception of radicalisation and terrorism. It's true. We often find ourselves at the mercy of events that we do not fully understand. And perhaps we do not even have the necessary means to analyse and fully comprehend phenomena that are so intricate. But excessive worry over terrorism might lead us to overestimate the true entity of support for violence in the name of God, promoting fearful prospects.

We should think about this. And should mend tones and narratives, avoiding making alarmist generalisations.

On its end, the Islamic community has much to take care of too. On the one hand, many participants (rightly) ask for more social, cultural and religious rights. They claim a place in the society they were born in or have been living in. In this respect, the type of commitment showed by certain workers, women, second-generations, and converts is simply commendable. And I believe these actors can truly help us establish a more inclusive society.

But on the other hand, there are real problems that undermine the good work by the actors I've just mentioned. Some individuals within the community demand respect, but they do not show any. Instead, they want to impose, judge and, where possible, change society according to their needs. That is, these people do not want to improve themselves and serve the country, but they want to change it from within. In doing so, they end up marginalising themselves and others, stigmatising groups that do not conform to specific visions or behaviours (women, homosexuals, Christians, former Muslims, Jews, Israelis, atheists ...).

Furthermore, a substantial minority continues to justify and glorify violence in the name of God. This kills every logic against terrorism and radicalisation carefully strategized and aimed at wider constituencies. It destroys years of hard-sought integration. And it increases suspicion over the whole Islamic community. Though a minority, Muslims accepting religious violence always outnumber non-Muslims in every examined case (violence in defence of faith, duty to punish offenders and support of Al Qaeda and ISIS).

What makes me hope is that both groups see integration and multiculturalism as key tools for a better future. And, perhaps, that is exactly what we should talk about next.

Are We the Next France?

Pondering over the dynamics of the controversial but fascinating encounters between Muslim and non-Muslim participants, I once again cannot help but ask myself: what should we do now? It is clear that we have much to work on, but where do we start from? How are we doing? Good? Bad? Compared to other countries, what are we doing? And, above all, where are we going?

In this sense, I often wonder if Italy could become the next France.

I think this is a fair question. After all, our French cousins share much with us. There are numerous social conditions that I consider discretely similar. And our two cultures, even if we don't want to admit it, have many common traits.

But there are also great differences, some of which immense - especially if one looks at the French Islamic community.

Still, can we be the next France?

In the short term, I do not believe so.

First, as already said, there are considerable differences. Our colonial past in Libya and in the Horn of Africa is nothing comparable to French imperial history. In modern times, Rome does not "boast" the same (positive or negative) experience Paris has in countries like Tunisia, Algeria, Morocco and Mali. Despite the fact the Islamic community is growing, the Muslims of Italy are less than half of those in France. In this regard, the vast majority of the Islamic community in Italy is composed of first-generation members who come from abroad; France, on the other hand, gives birth to third, fourth, and fifth-generation Muslim citizens. In fact, since immigration from Islamic countries is a relatively new phenomenon, Italian outskirts cannot be compared to the French banlieues of Saint-Denis and Marseille.

Furthermore, while Italy has yet to witness a large-scale attack, France is the most targeted European nation by jihadist terrorism - so to speak, the French count more than 70% of all the jihadist attacks put together by ISIS. French fighters have formed the Caliphate's largest European battalion, amounting to almost 3,000; our fighters, that is, those who are coming or who are connected in some way to Italy, are 125. And, finally, Italy does not yet seem to face certain social tensions spurring beyond the Alps. For the moment, beatings of Italian women in bikinis by gangs of Muslim girls have not been reported; nor have violent demonstrations outside the Israeli embassy or writings on French planes praising ISIS.

Ergo, in the short run, we can sleep soundly, for France appears far away.

That said, things could change.

In truth, there are several signs that we are trending precisely towards that direction. Al Qaeda and ISIS have not yet attacked us, but that does not mean that we are automatically safe. In reality, if we study the matter in question, our country *does* feature a pretty respectful jihadist record.

Well before the ISIS era, Italy is already a crossroads for terrorists. We host, in fact, members of Al Qaeda directly or indirectly linked to Osama Bin Laden. We act as a logistics base for terrorist cells responsible for planning attacks abroad. Individuals and organisations send large funds to various theatres of Jihad, sometimes exploiting drugs trafficking and illegal immigration. Others smuggle weapons and fake documents (passports). Finally, we send fighters (which we will later call foreign fighters) to Bosnia, Afghanistan, Iraq and, more recently, Syria.

The jihadist spectrum is not only projected outside Italy, however. Since 2001, our country has recorded almost 30 Jihadist-related cases. Among these, one could mention some of the more "spectacular" plots, such as the plan to release cyanide, hidden in cans of tomato, in the ventilation system at the American embassy in Rome. Or the attempt to hijack a ship filled with explosives and have it crash in the port of Naples. We could also recall a series of "demonstrative" acts and one unsuccessful carried out attack – the one by Mr. Mohammed Game in Milan in 2009, with the device exploding in his hand in front of the Santa Barbara Carabinieri Station. Even if Milan is the terrorists' favourite target, Rome is the most cited and threatened city by the propaganda of the Islamic State. Further, Italy counts hundreds of preventive expulsions against persons on account of Jihadism and threats to national security. Not to mention dozens of Imams and mosques who, over the years, glorify Jihad, martyrdom and violence in the name of God, preaching anti-systemic and anti-Semitic sentiments.

In other words, although Italy remains marginal on the jihadist radar, the future is not guaranteed. Its recent history shows that even our country cannot be defined as totally immune to Jihadist interests. If it is fair to commend the police and our legal system of prevention (expulsions), it is equally correct to recognise that an attack could shake the internal balance and, perhaps, bring us closer to the French and European case.

Furthermore, it is not even obvious that the climate of relative social tranquillity will remain untouched.

That's true. To date, we do not have the same suburbs as the French do. However, as my journey has showed me, we begin to glimpse the first sprouts of the Italian *banlieue*. Little by little, more and more Italians abandon peripheral areas around large centres, leaving new ghettos inhabited mainly by foreign citizens. Neighbourhoods such as Torpignattara in Rome, the area of via Padova in Milan or La Falchera in Turin, all of which are highly Islamic-concentrated areas, could be prototypes of this.

This trend is worrying. If ignored, realities that are already complicated by definition could turn into centres similar to the French ones, where crime spreads and, with it, resentment –which is fertile ground for every jihadist recruiter.

Moreover, the Italian society could struggle at meeting second generations' and immigrants' expectations. Born or arrived in Italy from problematic theatres, both actors in question rightly wish for a better future. Hence, considering potential economic recessions and alarming rates of youth unemployment (especially in certain regions), these subjects' inclusion becomes crucial, for the inability (or unwillingness) to satisfy their social and economic needs might eventually create alienation, identity crisis, and frustration. In turn, this could expose potentially vulnerable people to the jihadist message, causing severe social division - as there seems to be in certain parts of France.

The signal is clear enough. If not addressed, these potential challenges could lead us towards a future of uncertainty. We could find ourselves with alienated generations of young Muslims residing in the new Italian *banlieues*, which, given our history of jihadism, could become venues of radicalisation and terrorism. Just like in France.

Now, I am not an alarmist and I hope with all my heart that this never happens. However, I also believe that it is not wise to roll our thumbs and hope that everything goes well.

So, what can we do to avoid being the next France?

Obviously, there are two battlefields.

The first is the Italian Islamic community. To begin, those in charge within the community should enhance official Imam training courses. These, in turn, should be committed (as many do already) to the reduction of "Do-it-yourself Imams"; to the abolition of any planned attempt of Islamisation, as well as any intolerant or discriminatory attitude towards any group (Christians, Jews, Buddhists, atheists, homosexuals, women ...); to promotion of attitudes and narratives of peace, coexistence and integration; to the genuine and sincere knowledge of Italian society, whose values, principles and history are often unknown; to the marginalisation and reporting to the competent authorities of those subjects potentially at risk of radicalisation.

In this regard, it is of fundamental importance that whoever is in charge continues to clarify the role of violence within Islam. I know. Most Italian Muslims reject the use of force. But this, apparently, is not enough, for there are still too many individuals who justify it precisely in religious terms, using double standards featuring thousands of exceptions demonising someone. And, given my results, these numbers are probably ignored or hidden by the same community to avoid problems.

On the one hand, this is understandable. It is better to pretend not to see or minimise issues when it can be done. However, if the community's goal is to gain greater respect and recognition, an incorrect perception or the refusal to identify cases of radicalisation and support for violence in the name of God might eventually undermine its own credibility and aspirations.

And this is another point. The community should continue to question what these aspirations are.

If the objective is the creation of a European Islam, which can act as a bridge between the world and Italy, then the predominant message should be the search for shared commonalities. Creating cultural bridges. Encouraging women, converts, and second generations. Studying history, culture, religion, Italian, and European philosophy. Redefining Islam's place within society. Showing respect to be respected.

Only in this way, in my humble opinion, can the community obtain the much-sought entente with the Italian State.

Italy must do its part too, though. As with the Islamic community, us Italian non-Muslims should too ask ourselves what kind of society we want. If we are afraid to open up, because we do not know what awaits us or because we simply fear whoever is different, then let's say it openly. Let's not hide behind a veil of hypocrisy. Sometimes, shutting everything down is the right thing to do. Sometimes it is not.

If, however, we believe opening up is good, then we must be ready to accept that not everyone will think like us. That not everyone will talk like us. That not everyone will eat like us. That not everyone will be like us. But we must have faith that everyone will be willing to collaborate for the creation of a multicultural and cohesive country.

Nevertheless, during this process it is vital to define which aspects of culture can be criticised, changed, and improved (such as certain racist attitudes) and which aspects, instead, must be protected and safeguarded, for they are non-negotiable.

Having said this, if this is the goal, then society should, to the best of its ability, assist the Islamic community in its social integration. First, institutions should listen more to public malaise, affecting any religious, political, social orientation, applying their resources and energies to make sure every individual feels part of society.

In order to increase the Italian Muslims' sense of belonging, it is necessary to raise public awareness on issues that *all* citizens have in common. Avoiding the creation of a "Muslim question", striving for greater integration of all foreign communities; avoiding the establishment of ghettos inhabited only by foreigners; offering alternative narratives to potential feelings of abandonment and alienation; avoiding, even unconsciously, the stigmatisation of Muslims citizens (and foreigners in general), whose opinion is only taken into account after major attacks and never (or almost never) after a football match of the national team, for example.

To such regard, society should watch the tone the media and certain politicians utilise. Avoiding alarmism, generalisations and computer trolls. Remembering that we are too, historically, a population of migrants. Recalling that many of our ancestors have experienced what so many foreigners currently experience in Italy. But we must not be afraid to tell what is not working and which aspects of our culture and values are being minimised, for the latter must be defended and respected by everyone. Getting rid of what someone would label radical chic behaviours. In other words, finding balance to avoid polarisation.

Finally, the last note is for both parties. As in any team sport, the game cannot be won alone. Great individuals can be decisive, but in the end, it is the group that counts. We win together and lose together. Italian Muslims and Italian non-Muslims must team up and play together. And to do so, it is necessary to know each other. It is necessary to listen. It is necessary to think. It is necessary to train. Criticise. Even harshly, but always in a respectful and constructive way.

This is the challenge of our time. It is up to us to accept it or decline it.

Come on.

There's not only dark in the distance.

www.ingramcontent.com/pod-product-compliance
Lightning Source LLC
Chambersburg PA
CBHW030657230426
43665CB00011B/1132